A
North Africa Story

A
North Africa Story

The Anthropologist as OSS Agent 1941-1943

By CARLETON S. COON

*With Historical Settings
from the editors of Gambit*

1980

Gambit, IPSWICH, MASSACHUSETTS

First Printing

Library of Congress Cataloging in Publication Data

Coon, Carleton S.
    A North Africa Story

    SUMMARY: A diary-like account of behind the scenes es-
pionage by a US (OSS) agent in North Africa.
    1. World War, 1939–1945—Secret service—United
States. 2. World War, 1939–1945—Personal narratives,
American. 3. Coon, Carleton Stevens, 1904– 4. World
War, 1939–1945—Africa, North. 5. United States. Office of
Strategic Services—Biography. 6. Spies—United States—Bi-
ography. I. Gambit, Incorporated (Firm) II. Title
D810.S8C618   940.54'86'73   80–11997
ISBN 0–87645–108–3

Cloth   ISBN 0–87645–108–3

Printed in the United States of America.

On Learning of the death of

WILD BILL DONOVAN

Wild, people called him, who had heard of his fame
And wild he was in heart and in feyness
But more than wild was the man with the wile of Odysseus
Like the king of Assassins he welded together
An army of desperate, invisible soldiers
Each as bold as himself in single deeds
But none as keen as himself, the leader of all, commander of men
Who could ask, "Jim, will you limpet that ship?"
Knowing the answer, for none would refuse him, or
"Carl, a free ride to Albania?" "Yes? Then you're off,
Ten minutes to Zero," and we would all die for him.
Die for him some of us did, but he died for us all.
Some who are left would burn him whole, like a Viking jarl in his
        ship
Others would cover his bones with a colossal marble cross
Each to his taste, say I, Yankee, Irishman, Italian.
As many tombs will he have in our hearts as the scattered remains
        of Osiris,
How lucky we were that he came when he did in the long tide of
        history
Hail to Wild Bill, a hero of men and a name to hang myths on
As American as chowder, Crockett, and Putnam
A free fighter's hero, may God give him peace.

CARLETON S. COON

June 2, 1959

THE ACRONYMS

AC of S Assistant Chief of Staff

CIA   Central Intelligence Agency

COI   Coordinator of Information

CIC   Counter Intelligence Corps

DAD   Administration Politique (French)

G-2   Military Intelligence Division, War Department

G-3   Organization and Training Division

HQ   Headquarters (Common abbreviation)

JIC   Joint Intelligence Center

OSS   Office of Strategic Services

OWI   Office of War Information

Post IA Post Intelligence

PX   Post Exchange (soldiers' shop)

QM   Quartermaster's Corps

RAF   Royal Air Force (British)

SD   Special Detatchment

SI   Secret Intelligence (OSS)

SIS   Secret Intelligence Service (British)

SO   Special Operations (OSS)

SOE   Special Operations Executive (British)

W/T   Wireless telegraph (radio)

CONTENTS

[*vii*   ]

Contents

P R E F A C E

KNOWN throughout the world as a distinguished anthropologist, Carleton Coon has had a second career as a secret agent and adventurer not unlike that of the English writer Geoffrey Household. Along with others of outstanding ability and hardy temperament, Coon joined the OSS* after the outbreak of the Second World War and served General William Donovan on a succession of missions and assignments until he received Donovan's letter of farewell and gratitude in September 1945. The personal narrative presented here deals with events in North Africa from before the Allied landings until the fall of Tunisia in May 1943.

By all accounts, not only this one, life in the OSS appears to have had a character all its own. Coon describes it by saying, "I never took an oath for the COI or OSS. We were all gentleman volunteers on our honor. We were never under orders. We were always asked, "Would you like to . . . (e.g., get yourself killed)?" To which we always said "yes."

That feeling comes clearly through this account. Not remarkable for any secret it discloses, it is noteworthy for the sense of immediacy it conveys, for its picture of people doing astonishing and dangerous things in an ordinary manner, and as a rare glimpse into an agent's mind while he is on the job, or at any rate what he feels he can set down about it.

* Actually then the COI—Coordinator of Information. Well along in 1942 the COI was divided into the Office of Strategic Services (OSS) and the Office of War Information (OWI). The OSS was disbanded in late September 1945.

Taken from indelible memories and dictated in two sessions in the first six months of 1943, the words of this story are adjacent in time to the deeds they describe. Coon wrote this as reports to headquarters, but also for his own enjoyment. The manner is casual and humorous, but the tension shows, particularly in the full-dress character studies in Part IV. Throughout, Coon is surprisingly free with comment and intensely security-conscious, although he never mentions the word. These seeming contradictions produce a narrative of startling and vivid detachment, as though the author were offset in some way from the purpose of the mission for which he is risking his life. It may have helped to feel that way sometimes.

Born and raised north of Boston, Massachusetts, Carleton Coon went to Harvard, where he studied anthropology under Earnest Hooton. That was in the early Twenties, and he became intrigued, as did Professor Hooton, by reports of supposedly nordic African tribes, under a leader named Abd el-Krim, who were fighting Spain for their independence. Coon determined that he would solve the scientific problem of the Riffians.

This curiosity, which he did not hide, led to a meeting in his rooms with an athletic young man named Gordon H. Browne, who, although not a scientist, felt a strong pull from the direction of Africa. These two young men hit it off well together and went to Morocco by way of France in the summer of 1924. On that try, they didn't get into the Rif country in the manner of Vincent Sheean, or in any manner at all, but they came close, traveled a lot, and saw enough to turn their interest into addiction. They also transformed their acquaintanceship into lasting friendship.

Several years and a number of journeys later, Browne went to live in Morocco as the resident partner of a Boston importing company. For his part, Coon kept going back professionally and finally got into the Rif lands on his third trip in 1926. That was a particularly arduous and hazardous expedition, on which his new *wife fearlessly accompanied him. From then on, with intervals out for teaching and writing, Coon roamed the length and breadth of Spanish Morocco, taking anthropological measurements of the tribespeople, making friends with them and their chiefs, reinforcing his knowledge of their languages and dialects, and becoming familiar with the paths and trails through the mountains. By 1939 he had as thorough a knowledge of the country and its people as any Westerner.*

When war broke out in Europe, both Browne, who soon returned to the United States, and Coon expected the American government to send them into North Africa on certain missions in preparation for what they considered inevitable American participation. Nothing of the sort was done. Month after month passed, and they waited with what patience they could, doing odd jobs for Army Intelligence. One of these was both large and important, the preparation of an English-Arabic phrase book for the troops who might someday use it. After the booklet was approved, and then edited by the scholar and poet Leonard Bacon, it eventually proved extremely useful. Meanwhile, and at last, in the spring of 1942, Browne and Coon entered the COI, underwent separately special training in communications, explosives, and weapons, and left for North Africa under (in Coon's case) reluctantly granted State Department cover.

To avoid confusion, the historical settings by the editors are set in a modified-italic face as is this preface. These may thus easily be distinguished from the work itself.

MARK SAXTON
FOR THE EDITORS

Ipswich
Spring, 1980

[*xi*]

A
North Africa Story

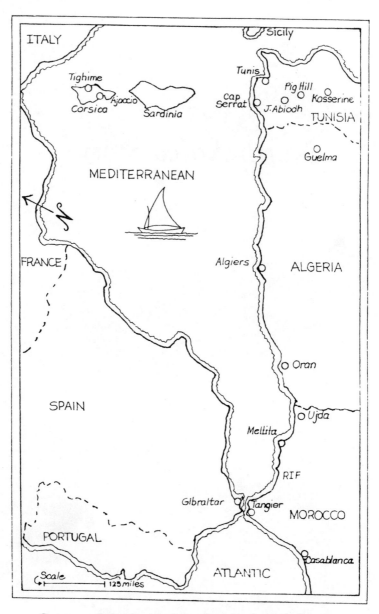

Scenes of Action in North Africa and Corsica

CHAPTER ONE

Before the Beginning

Joining the OSS

SINCE childhood I have wanted to do the kind of work I have been doing for the past year. There should be nothing unusual in this; it is probably the secret ambition of every boy to travel in strange mountains, stir up tribes, and destroy the enemy by secret and unorthodox means. Most boys, however, grow up, and as they adjust themselves to civilized living this ambition usually dies.

In my particular case, I think my family and friends will be all too quick to agree, I have never in this sense, at least, completely grown up, and I have been able to fill in the period between boyhood and warfare by alternative tasks that permitted this ambition to survive. In brief, I became a field anthropologist before I left college, and in the twenty years between my beginning this life and my service with the government I was able to make eight field trips to North Africa, Albania, Russia, Ethiopia, and Arabia, and to spend the rest of my time in related teaching and research.

My last field trip was to Morocco in 1939, with my wife and two sons; Harvard University gave me a half sabbatical that year after five years of uninterrupted teaching and writing. I chose Morocco on this occasion because, like everyone else, I knew that another World War was inevitable, and because it seemed to me that Morocco might become an important theater. I had not been there for eleven years and wanted to renew my acquaintance with the country and the people.

We found the country strangely quiet and apathetic; although I concentrated on archaeological work, I spent as much time as possible renewing my knowledge of the local Arabic and my old relationships with natives. We got out on a Danish freighter late in August, and arrived home a few days before Britain declared war on Germany. At this time several of us who had done field work in unusual places and who spoke unusual languages teamed together to find some way to serve the Allied governments, but we had little luck. Captain Gordon Browne was one of this group from the beginning, for he had had much experience in Morocco and knew parts of the country with which I was unacquainted.

Our first step was to tackle G-2 through its Boston office; we received a polite brush-off. Then one of our group, Patrick Putnam, who lived in the Belgian Congo, got in touch with Colonel Sharp of the New York G-2 office, and through him first Browne and then I made Colonel Sharp's acquaintance. Up until the time I left in May 1942, I worked unofficially for Colonel Sharp, digging out maps and documents, getting together photographs, finding people who spoke Japanese, checking on local people whom he wanted investigated, etc. Although he appreciated this work, Colonel Sharp was unable to find a way to send either Browne or myself to North Africa.

In the spring of 1941 Gordon Browne had the idea of preparing a handbook and dictionary for North Africa for the use of American troops should they ever go there; we wrote this and sent it to Sharp, who had us send another copy to Leonard Bacon of the Military Dictionary Committee. In modified form, this handbook was later printed and given to the invasion army at the time of the landing.

About this same time Colonel Sharp sent Browne to see Lieutenant Ambrose Chambers in his New York office. There Browne also met Mr. Phillips. Lieutenant Chambers and Mr. Phillips told Browne that they were looking for men who spoke French to go to Casablanca as food-control officers. They explained that the job would consist of checking food shipments and nothing else; there would be neither intelligence work nor operations. They said that they would consider both Browne and me. Browne told them that if there were to be no intelligence or operations, and no contact with Moslems, he would decline both for himself and for me. Thus we failed to get in with the first batch of control vice-consuls, including Wilkes, Canfield, Pendar, King, Culbert, Reid, and Bartlett, who went out a year before we did. Personally I am pleased that it worked out as it did, because I was able to finish my textbook, *Principles of Anthropology*, upon which I was working, and when I did go out, I was able to go with OSS training, which I would have otherwise missed.

In September a British agent wrote Browne, asking to see him; a Major Sinclair wanted him to come to New York and discuss the idea that he should go to Casablanca under commercial cover to work for them. Browne asked Mr. Phillips whether he should accept this or not, and Mr. Phillips replied that he would handle the matter. As it later appeared, Mr. Phillips did nothing about it and Major Sinclair did not know why Browne had failed to answer him, but later, Browne met Sinclair, with profitable results.

About this time Mr. Phillips wanted Browne to go out under naval cover, and told him to apply for a commission in the navy. Consequently Browne filled out all the blanks, took his examinations, and the lengthy process of getting him a commission began. Then, on the day of the Harvard-Yale football game, 1941, Mr. Phillips came to Cambridge and interviewed me in my office. He told me to get a naval commission as well. Unlike Browne, I failed the physical examination. The grounds were obesity and gross overweight, and hypertension. None of these conditions exists today.

During all this, the day of Pearl Harbor arrived, and Mr. Phil-

[5   ]

lips, like everyone else in the government, became extremely busy. I went to Washington to see Mr. Phillips. He tried to have me sent as a vice-consul, but the State Department turned me down. It seemed that in 1933 the Honorable Addison B. Southard, American minister to Ethiopia, had turned in an unfavorable report on my activities in that country, and I was on the State Department black list. Nothing could be done unless I could find another cover.

I went home and made tentative arrangements to be accredited as a correspondent for the North American Newspaper Alliance, but Mr. Phillips vetoed that. Then in desperation I went to New York to see Major Sinclair, whom Mr. Phillips had told Browne not to see. Major Sinclair went to Washington the next day to see Colonel Solborg about me, and Colonel Solborg sent for me at once. Browne was there; he had already been accepted as a vice-consul; Mr. Phillips had told him not to accept his naval commission which had just come through. This caused considerable embarrassment and some hard feeling in the Boston naval office.

Solborg led Browne and myself into his private office, and asked us if we were willing to go to Morocco, make contacts with the Riffian tribes, and hide out in the mountains when the Germans came in. We agreed. Then I told Colonel Solborg about the State Department's attitude toward me, and he spoke to Mr. Phillips. Mr. Phillips slid his glasses halfway down his nose, looked at me over the lenses, and said, "I will fix that." He did. How he persuaded the State Department brahmins and pharisees to relent, I do not know.

Colonel Solborg went to Lisbon; I became a member of SO under Colonel Goodfellow. Browne left for Morocco. Colonel Goodfellow sent me to school in Canada. On May 7 I went to New York to take the *Clipper*, left on the 11th, and arrived in Lisbon on the 12th. Here I was held over for two weeks, for the State Department had changed its mind and cabled that I was to be immobilized in Lisbon indefinitely.

[6   ]

In Lisbon one minor event took place which I recount without rancor, and only because it may serve to illustrate the attitude of the State Department toward us in the earlier part of the war. That attitude has since, I trust, been changed. Having been told that newcomers in Lisbon were carefully watched by the enemy, it occurred to me that since I was under State Department cover I should make some pretense of working for that department. So I went to the Embassy and saw Mr. Millard, the counselor of Embassy, and asked him if there was some room in the Embassy where I could sit and read books, keeping out of people's way; his reply was a classic: "Go and bask on the beach of Estoril. I serve my government and am proud of it. You are, I suppose, serving your government, too. So, in a sense, you really have nothing to be ashamed of. We have no room for you here."

I spent most of my time in Lisbon acting as coding clerk for Colonel Solborg and Lieutenant Chambers. I was careful not to be seen with the former in public since I was told that he had been spotted. From what I have since seen of German efficiency, I know now that this care was probably unnecessary.

Finally I received a wire signed with that magic name HULL instructing me to proceed to my post, which I did, arriving May 27 in Tangier, where I was greeted by Colonel Eddy. I had met Colonel Eddy in Washington in December, in Mr. Phillips' office. I had wanted to speak to him privately, and he had wanted to speak to me, but that had been impossible. Now I was to begin an association with a person whom I consider one of the greatest men I have ever met, one of the happiest associations of my life.

CHAPTER TWO

The "Torch" Operation

Historical Setting: May to November 1942

THE OSS mission in North Africa was defined by the decisions taken at the Arcadia Conference in Washington in January 1942. There the Anglo-American Allies gave Germany first priority among their enemies and decided that landings on French Africa that fall would be the best employment of the limited forces they would then have ready. The new armies in the West, in concert with the British Eighth Army based on Alexandria, would crush the Axis forces between them. This would recover control of the Mediterranean, shorten global supply lines, and open up the famous "soft underbelly" of Europe to which Churchill liked to refer when he didn't want to talk about the coast of France.

Prior to the landings, the OSS made its headquarters in Tangier in the International Zone, some thirty-seven miles southwest of Gibraltar. The Zone's administration had been taken over by Spain in 1940 simultaneously with the fall of France. During this period, the overall job of the OSS was to ensure that the landings were unopposed or, failing that, to keep resistance light, and to guard against interference from Spanish territory. This involved a wide range of dealings, some of them inherently at cross-purposes, with local French authorities across the border, Free French soldiers, colons (colonials of French, Spanish, and Italian origins), urban and coastal Arabs and Berbers, and the warlike tribes of the interior. Many forms of undercover activity including the operation of secret radio networks, the smuggling of arms, and building reliable connections with the natives were of great importance.

Coon describes his anomalous position in the consulate general in Tangier and his real job as courier between Gibraltar and Africa, part of which was smuggling arms and equipment. High, if not first, on his list of concerns was the danger from Spain. It was thought then that it was touch-and-go whether Franco would join the Axis outright or at least allow German troops free passage through his territory. It is known today that Franco had no intention of willingly doing either, but the evidence was strong on the other side. Spain was a fascist state and Franco came to power with armed support from Hitler and Mussolini. He had taken Tangier at the first chance, and Gibraltar was a thorn in his side. There was a large German presence in Spain and Spanish Morocco with important facilities and privileges. All this was given additional color when, as anticipated, German troops took over the rest of France—Vichy France, all the way to the Spanish border a few days after the Allied North African landings. Hence Coon's and Browne's deep and profitable involvement with Tassels, who had been Abd el-Krim's minister in charge of weapons, military supplies, and recruitment, and with Strings, a powerful religious leader, and the followers of both, most of whom were as hostile to France as they were to Spain.

Preparations for the Landing

COVER JOB

WHEN I arrived in Tangier I did not, of course, know that American troops were going to land in North Africa. I did not know that for several months, and I did not know the exact date until D-14, when I was told by a British colleague. But I did know that I was there to prepare for military eventualities and that my probable job was to make things hot for the Germans if and when they should move westward from Egypt and Tripoli.

In the meantime it was my duty to pretend to be a member of the State Department and to allay the curiosity of the legitimate or career personnel, who from the beginning viewed us irregulars with suspicion. I was supposed to serve as special assistant to the Legation, and no one knew exactly what that meant. Therefore I had to whittle out a cover job under that title.

Mr. Childs, the *chargé d'affaires* ad interim, knew that I was working for the COI, and lost no time in making that knowledge general among the staff. So he asked me what branch of the COI, and I said, the research and propaganda branch, and that I would, if he liked, busy myself with Arab affairs, to find out what the Arabs were thinking and how they could best be influenced. From the beginning my relations with Mr. Childs were cordial and we had but two minor brushes, one of which I will relate presently and the second when he refused to let Browne and myself put CD (Corps Diplomatique) plates on our car. We were using the car for undercover work, and the legitimate State Department men could have these plates on their cars, which they were using for picnics and bathing parties. We kept a set of those plates under the seat, and used them when we were away from Tangier.

Upon my first interview with Mr. Childs he called in Paul Geier, who had charge of publishing the Legation bulletin in English, French, Spanish, and Arabic; in front of Geier he asked me to read an Arabic newspaper. When I failed to do this he said, with surprise, "I was told that you knew Arabic." I explained that I had not studied classical, printed Arabic for some years, and that the best I could do was to converse on simple subjects with the local natives, but that I would take lessons to remedy this deficiency.

Browne, who was not known to be working for COI, had been

sent to Casablanca as a coding clerk; however, Mr. Murphy and Colonel Eddy had him recalled to Tangier to collaborate with me. Together we worked out a forty-page compendium on the subject of Propaganda in Morocco, weaving into it an analysis of Moorish society in the two zones, in tribal areas and cities, and the ways to influence this society. Structurally I leaned heavily on my *Principles of Anthropology,* and padded it with enough technical terms to make it ponderous and mysterious, since I had found out in the academic world that people will express much more awe and admiration for something complicated which they do not quite understand than for something simple and clear. Mr. Childs expressed great admiration for this work, but refused to let us send it to the COI office; in fact, he refused to let us have any direct communication, but we sent it by hand undercover. Later he had it copied and sent it to the State Department with an introduction of his own, and after making us perform a number of corrections and omissions. I believe that the OSS now has a copy of each version.

In compiling this colossus, Browne and I made ample use of the profound knowledge of Morocco of Mr. Randolph Mohammed Gusus, about whom a few lines may be useful. Gusus, fifty-three, was born in Manchester, England, of a Moorish father and an English mother. He came back to Fez, his father's home, as a child, and was brought up as an Arab. Later he went to the States where he sold Moroccan leather goods, with an office in Boston, and he lived during this period next door to me and across the street from Browne, in Cambridge. In Morocco he also worked with Browne at various times. Before we went to Morocco in 1942, he was working for the British SIS, but they considered him of little worth and gladly relinquished him to us. This transfer was arranged by Browne, before his departure, through Major Sinclair. We later found that Gusus was a priceless agent, and that the SIS objected to him merely because he could not spell English properly in his written reports. Browne found Gusus a house in Tangier, got him native guards, and we had him employed by the Legation as a translator, which office he still fills.

At our first meeting, Mr. Childs asked me to take over the Arabic news bulletin from Geier, and later he wanted me to take charge of the distribution of all bulletins other than through the mail. That is, I was to distribute all the Arabic bulletins, and to distribute the European-language ones, through all channels except the mail, which duty Geier retained. Needless to say, these arrangements did not please Geier, and I do not blame him. I felt rather cheap to take over merely as a cover job something on which he had worked hard and in which he took pride, and I did my best to placate him and to praise him, particularly since he had done an admirable job.

Mr. Childs imposed numerous restrictions, which he changed from time to time; we were to distribute nothing in the French Zone, and our distribution in Tangier and the Spanish Zone was alternately forbidden and permitted by Mr. Childs as the Spaniards let the Germans distribute their material—every time the Spaniards let the Germans get away with something, Mr. Childs would dash to General Orgaz and demand an equal privilege. Browne, Gusus, and I soon discovered the futility of ordinary printed propaganda, but we had to pretend that we thought it was hot stuff in order to keep up our cover job.

Mr. Childs set me the task of finding out how influential our propaganda was in Tangier. Browne and I spent two days going from shop to shop visiting native friends and acquaintances, and discovered that none of them had ever seen or heard of the bulletin. We asked how it was being distributed, and Geier said that he gave several hundred copies a week to Mohammed, the head Shaoush, who slipped them under doorsills and in mailboxes, in the dark of night.

I said that Mohammed could not have been doing this since none had been read by a fair sample of the shopkeepers. Mr. Childs then said, "We will get to the bottom of this; send Mohammed Shaoush in." Mohammed came in, and Mr. Childs said: "Dr. Coon says that you have not been distributing your bulletins at all, and that no one has heard of them. How do you account for this?" Mohammed put on a toothy grin, and replied, "Well, Dr. Coon is new here and knows nothing about the natives; of course they would not admit to him that they had seen them." "So you see," said Mr. Childs to me, and dismissed Mohammed. That settled it as far as Mr. Childs was concerned.

A few minutes later I got Mohammed in a quiet place and gave him a hearty sock on the jaw. I should not, in theory, have done this, but from then on he did not interfere with my affairs. He was either destroying the bulletins, or turning them over to the Germans. We know that he saw the Germans frequently, but whether or not he gave them the bulletins we could not determine. We never found out what he did with them.

One of the few useful things we did in this cover job was to translate the President's Flag Day speech into Arabic. Browne and I would reword the English in a more Arabic-sounding way, and Gusus would sing out an Arabic poetical version and then write it down. Every time Mr. Roosevelt mentioned God once, we named Him six times; and the result was a piece of poetry that might have come out of the Koran. It was a free translation, but it caught Mr. Roosevelt's sense perfectly, and the original English lent itself well to this treatment. Finally we had it checked by the British Arabic expert at their Legation, and gave it to Geier to have several thousand copies printed. We mailed it all over the Spanish Zone, and some copies got (by mistake) into the French Zone. There the French announced that any native found with it in his possession would receive three months imprisonment.

Since the landing, this document has been read several times over the Rabat radio. More than anything else it gave the natives the idea that we would come across the sea to set them free; this influenced many of them in our favor, particularly those who had been wavering in an Axis direction, and it was very hard to explain to these natives, after the landing, why their condition had not immediately changed for the better.

Gusus, Browne, and I also supplied the Legation once or twice a week with translations of leading or significant articles in the Arab press; we would astound Mr. Childs with virulent attacks on Nogues, demands for a better radio program from Radio Tetuan, plaints against the pitiful black-market conditions of Tangier, etc. We also handed in a periodical scandal sheet of rumors from the Socco Chico, that rumor center of North Africa. Any other intelligence we received from our undercover sources and considered safe for State Department consumption was submitted in the same manner. In other words, we managed to make Mr. Childs think that these duties were occupying all of our time, and in fact they did equal about as much time-energy as the legitimate officials were producing.

In general the British found that their printed propaganda was as useless as ours.* They had bales of funny books and cartoons that the Arabs either could not understand or did not consider funny. Just as we had one successful issue, the President's speech, so they had one, a beautifully printed Ramadan greeting card made up in London, with red and gold and green Moorish designs. They gave us hundreds of these to distribute, as we gave them hundreds of copies of the President's speech.

We had one stroke of luck which Mr. Childs was quick to appreciate, and in which he was quick to cooperate, but he did not realize the extent to which we were fortunate. It seems that the most powerful religious brotherhood in Northern Morocco, which we will call the Strings organization, has its seat in Tangier, just as Mary Baker Eddy's organization has its Mother Church in Boston. The divine leader we will call Mr. Strings. He is a living God, and tens of thousands of fighting men all over the Spanish Zone and in parts of the French Zone will obey his orders blindly

---

* So did the Germans with theirs. Sourenhol complains about this in a letter taken from an intercepted German pouch.

to the death. It is as formidable an organization as the medieval Assassins.

Now Mr. Strings wanted cash to build a new wing on his Mother Mosque. The Spanish government had promised it several times, but never produced the money. So Mr. Strings sent a circular letter to the heads of all legations asking for contributions, and Mr. Childs sent me his copy of the letter. I told Mr. Childs that this seemed a priceless opportunity, and that I would like to go as his representative. I went, and Mr. Strings received me very graciously. After a little sparring he said that he had been accused by the Spaniards and Germans of working with us, and that put the idea into his head. By this circular letter he could get me to visit him openly and we could talk. I agreed to give him 50,000 francs, and he agreed to put his organization at the service of the United States government, for intelligence, for propaganda, and for armed revolt among all the tribes of the Ghomara confederacy, and many of those of the Jebala.

I went back to Mr. Childs and said that Mr. Strings needed money, and that a gift of this nature would create much good will for America among the tribes of Northern Morocco; that it would be our prime coup in the propaganda field. Mr. Childs, who accepted this idea enthusiastically, gave me 20,000 francs of State Department money. I took 30,000 more out of the naval attaché's safe, from the COI funds, since Mr. Strings had said that he needed 50,000. From that time on Mr. Strings was our man, as will be shown in later sections of this discourse. Browne was away at the time, but he was introduced to Mr. Strings later, and after I had left Tangier he took complete charge of our relations with the Strings organization.* I also found out later that it was Gusus who

---

* Major Brooker, in his lectures on subversive organization, told us never to hook up with pre-existing associations as they are too easily penetrated. I offer our experience with the Strings brotherhood as an example to the contrary.

had had the brilliant idea of the circular letter, and had passed this on to Mr. Strings through an intermediary.

Later on, shortly before D-day, Mr. Childs received word that COI had ceased to exist, that part had gone over to OWI and part to OSS. He asked me what part I was to be in, if any, or whether this ended my mission. I said that I did not know the answer, but presumed that I would stay on as OWI. I begged him to let the matter rest until definite instructions had been received. So it did rest until after the landing, when he of course discovered what organization I worked for.

I must say that considering the way that I constantly deceived Mr. Childs, and asked him permission to make what seemed to him senseless trips, and apparently violated State Department codes of behavior, he was extraordinarily tolerant. When I wrote him from Algiers, upon the eve of my departure from North Africa, that I had deeply appreciated my period of tenure on his staff, I meant what I said. He held no resentment against us for not having told him in advance about the landing, which took him completely by surprise. Despite everything that happened, I feel that my relationship with Mr. Childs was eminently satisfactory, and I am pleased that he considers me a friend.

SUBVERSIVE ORGANIZATION

BEFORE D-day, this activity was shared equally by Gordon Browne and myself; after D-day, it became uniquely Browne's concern and he maintained it through the difficult period between November 8 and May 8, the fall of Tunisia. When I left North Africa he had the even more difficult job of calling off the watchdogs and ensuring their safety—a job, at this writing, he is still doing.

Our purpose in organizing subversive groups in Spanish Morocco was to prevent the Germans from taking this country in the event that they (a) moved west from Tripoli or (b) moved south through Spain. Later on we added to this the purpose of facilitating the success of American and British arms in case the United Nations should make a landing in International or Spanish territory, or both, or in case the Spaniards should try to close the Straits of Gibraltar. The British SOE had much the same idea, but early in the game we agreed on a division of labor whereby the British would handle Christians in Tangier and Spaniards in Morocco, and we Moslems. Their plans with Gibraltareans, Spanish Reds, and dissident Hungarians and Yugoslavs were well laid, and still are. It was up to us to do equally well with the Moslems.

Our first fruitful contact in this field was with Tassels. He was a general, in charge of recruitment and supplies, in Abd el Krim's army, and is still one of the most influential leaders, undercover, in the Rif. He came to Tangier periodically to compare notes about business with Gusus, since he had established himself as a wealthy and prominent merchant in Tetuan. Browne and I first met him in June, and held monthly meetings from that time onward.

It was not easy to arrange meetings with Tassels, since he is a well-known man and if he should be seen with us by the Spanish or anyone in contact with the Spanish, he would be shot. He was well aware of this and did his best to keep these meetings secret. The usual system was for Gusus to see him by coincidence in the Tingis café, where both habitually sat at noontime, to eat lunch and drink coffee. There Gusus would slip him the details of the rendezvous. These were always nocturnal. Browne and I would get out the car, or if possible borrow some other car for variety. We would be at a prearranged place on a lonely street at a prearranged hour, and would see Tassels walking along. If no one was about, we would stop and get him quickly into the back seat; if there were too many people around, we would come back and pick him up a few minutes later.

Once in the car we would transform him. Sometimes we would

turn him into a Fatma, or Arab woman, with a veil. Other times we would turn him into a shaush, with a tall fez on his head garnished with the US seal in gold metal, or the naval attaché's seal—thus we were merely taking one of our servants to a villa to wait on a cocktail party. Later we would shift him to a Spaniard, putting a European hat on his head, and a European coat over him. We never were able to eliminate the baggy trousers, but when we got out of the car we would walk beside him so that these would not be visible.

We shifted our meeting place as often as possible. Sometimes we saw him in Colonel Eddy's villa on the mountain, where we kept the Midway radio set; sometimes at el Farhar Pension, a hotel run by an American, Winthrop Buckingham; sometimes in the home of an obliging British lady, Mrs. Bertram Thomas. Once when we were to meet him at Mrs. Thomas's, I was stationed to lie under the rose bushes near the entrance to her garden, to lead him in when he should appear at the gate. Colonel Eddy, Mrs. Thomas, and Browne were on the roof. I lay in the bushes next to a reed fence, and spiders and ants crawled over me and spun webs over me. Meanwhile a pair of Spanish lovers lay down on the other side of the fence; I was treated to all their physiological noises as well as their periodic and inane conversation. Finally, after what seemed to me a distinguished effort (compared to the graph on sexual intercourse published by Boaz and Goldschmitt in "The Heart Rate," *American Journal of Physiology*), they left, and I was able to move and brush off a few cobwebs. I retired to the roof and Gordon made a sortie, finally picking up Tassels, who was wandering about lost several blocks away.

On another occasion Browne, Gusus, and I shepherded Tassels to el Farhar. The plan was that Gusus, Tassels, and I were to hide on the steps leading to the upper garden. Browne was to drive on to the office, where Buckingham would see him. Browne was then to proceed to the lower cottage to make sure that the coast was clear, and return for Buckingham, and together they were to join us by the upper path. It was pitch dark. Browne left as planned. Tassels thought he saw a Spaniard behind a tree, and I stalked this spectre with a .45. Something went wrong, for at that moment Buckingham, leaving his desk, had crept along the upper path, and he fell over Tassels and Gusus with a loud crash. No one cried out, but when I got there I found Gusus and Buckingham wrestling in silence. Tassels had passed out from a blow on the head. Gusus had a swollen nose and Buckingham had an egg-size lump on the head. Browne appeared and we resuscitated Tassels. Meanwhile Tassels' Spaniard had been a lump on the side of a tree. We took Tassels to the lower cottage and applied first aid to the three injured members of the party, after which Buckingham retired to the porch to guard, and the rest of us proceeded with our conversation.

Tassels always had a lot to say. We were the only people he could talk with, and so we had a month's stored-up interaction to cope with at each meeting. Sometimes he talked for four or five hours without a break. After the second hour I usually became bored and had to walk around, but Browne sat through it stoically and took notes. During these meetings Tassels gave us much combat intelligence, battle order, troop movements, etc., in great detail, and most of this we passed on to Colonel Johnson, the military attaché, who sent it on to G-2 in Washington. Most of it checked with other sources; it was seldom that Tassels was inaccurate.

During these meetings we laid our plans for the revolt of the Riffians if needed, and plotted the landing of troops, the dropping of parachutists, the delivery of guns, the cutting off of roads and garrisons, etc. We laid on a system of signals by which the Riffians were to assemble and seize various key positions, and to await our arrival; all these plans were submitted to General Donovan and are on record in the OSS office. After the landing, Browne and I consulted with Tassels on the one hand and General Clark on the other; we laid on a new scheme by which we were to enter the Rif from the South overland in case the Germans should come through Spain. Only after the fall of Tunis did these plans become obsolete.

Our other subversive planning was with the Strings group, who were to do for the western Spanish Zone what Tassels and his gang were to do for the Rif. These plans were equally elaborate and also took many meetings. Sometimes we talked with Strings himself, and he arranged our meetings in his holy of holies with great secrecy; the streets were cleared by his henchmen, who silently handed us on from corner to corner, and did the same on the way out. On other occasions we talked with his number one man, Idris. Neither Tassels nor Strings knew of the other, but we took care that their plans did not overlap.

With Strings as with Tassels, we devised alternate plans for the period from November 8, 1942, to May 8, 1943. Strings even more than Tassels furnished us with intelligence, and laid on alternate plans—he was prepared to hide us out in case the Germans surprised us in Tangier, to hide other Europeans for us, and to engineer the escape of the American parachutists from concentration in Sheshawen. Fortunately we did not have to make use of any of these services.

A third group with whom we had conversations was the Moroccan Nationalist Party. This is a complex organization with many splits and ramifications. The main group was centered in Fez under its ghazi, Allal el Fasi. In 1936 the French deported Fasi to Brazzaville, and forced the party underground. Hamid Belafrej, another leader, went to Tangier; Si Hamid Mekkwar, still another, was allowed to remain in Fez as long as he did nothing active. Abd el Khalek Torres and Mekki Nasiri went to Tetuan where they were encouraged by Colonel Beigbeder. When Beigbeder was replaced by General Orgaz, they too were discouraged, and went into German pay.

At Tangier I had a conversation with Belafrej, who outlined the aims of the party. They realize that they cannot get the French out. Like almost all North Africans, they despise the French for taking away their lands and privileges and treating them as inferiors. Yet they knew that the French are firmly entrenched and that they cannot live without them. So what they want is political equality, relief from economic exploitation, and above all *the opportunity for education.* They want to become modern people, like the Turks and Iranians and other Moslems who realize that the Moslem Middle Ages are over, and they know that the key to this change is education.

The French (and I have heard many of them say this) think that the Moroccans are not sufficiently "evolved" for education of modern life. I have not been told what theory of evolution this idea stems from, but it sounds something like Montandon's theory of Ologenesis, one of the false doctrines of fascist science the germs of which were developed in Italy early in the Mussolini period by a pseudoscientist named Rosa. Montandon carried it over to France, and elaborated it; Ologenesis may well have influenced Hitler in his garbled notions of a *herrenvolk.*

At any rate, it gives the French a rationalization for their treatment of the natives as inferiors. The nastier French say that the natives are like beasts; the more kindly ones say that they are like children. No Frenchman whom I have met, among scientists, soldiers, colonists, or whatever, will admit that the natives, if properly educated and trained, are their intellectual equals; but they cannot be too sure of this theory because they are afraid to put it to the test.

Belafrej and all the others are primarily motivated not by economics, not by politics, not by religion, but by the fact that *the French treat them as social inferiors.* This rankles them constantly and they rationalize in their turn, using religion frequently as an excuse, and also, quite correctly, pointing out that equality of education would in time do the trick.

In Fez I held a secret meeting with Mekkwar, and the French secret police, despite their boasting to me later that they knew every place I visited and every person I had talked with, did not know that I had met Mekkwar. They do not know it yet. Hamid the Jackal, one of Browne's old retainers, led me to the rendezvous by a tortuous route, called the "Jackal's trail," by which we shook off all tails.

Mekkwar said almost the same things that Belafrej had said in Tangier. He was more on the religious side, and was also rather stuffy. He disapproved of all religious brotherhoods and wanted to purge Islam, after the manner of Ibn Saud. He said that the Germans had approached him but that he would not play with them. I believe this, but the French do not. They are convinced that the Nationalists of Fez were hand in glove with the Armistice Commission.

At any rate, Browne and I came to the conclusion that the Nationalists, however honorable they might be and however worthy their ambitions and ideals, were not men of action. They were great talkers and mystics, hard to pin down to facts. They had had enough European education to make them restless, but not enough to let them know how to act in either a native or a modern sense. Since we were interested only in action, we would do much better to confine our attention to the men from the hills, the men who knew how to handle not the inkpot but the rifle. Therefore we concentrated on our undercover friends in the North, and left the dreamers alone.

Tassels and Strings and their associates worked for us 100 percent and risked their lives in so doing. As long as the Spaniards remain in Morocco their activities cannot be revealed. As long as they are there we can count on them as loyal friends, although Tassels is a bit disgusted with us for not having taken Spanish Morocco, and he told Browne, "If you come through the Rif after this, even the little children will throw stones at you." We organized these revolts as prophylactic measures. I was prepared to leave Gibraltar on November 7 with a landing party bound for Ajdir—I had a Riffian costume with me for that purpose. Later

Browne and I were prepared to enter the Rif in jeeps, I through Boured—Tizi Ifri—he through Suk el Had of Agadir el Krush. The need of these expeditions never arose, and we will never know what degree of success we would have had.

INTELLIGENCE WORK

A side issue of our preinvasion work was straight intelligence, which cannot, in our experience, be completely divorced from operations. Our first efforts were relatively unproductive. Gusus transmitted all the stories that were going the Moslem rounds, and fou 'd a few informants in the Mixed Court and elsewhere, but w' ɔon had better use for him than to collect such items. One of our earliest agents was the Big Moh, a Riffian who worked in the jail and had the keys to the cells; he was willing to let the prisoners out whenever we should be ready—that is, whenever a landing was to be made, and civil disturbance might be needed. In the meantime, he handed us a weekly list of all prisoners, and when a new victim arrived whom he thought important, he made a special trip to tell us. In this way we learned of the arrest of one of Mr. Child's informants, a Captain Carranza, before anyone else. Big Moh's usefulness was limited and specialized, and we did not try to use him for anything else.

Another early agent was Mr. Fish, a sharîf who spoke English; he was an elderly and respected shopkeeper. We sent him to Ceuta to buy some goods for his shop, and gave him a $50 bonus. Colonel Johnson agreed to pay us the $50 if we would give him the information collected, which we did, and the G-2 red tape kept Colonel Johnson waiting several weeks before he got the $50 from Washington, at which point we thanked God for the freedom from red tape in our own organization. Mr. Fish collected certain combat intelligence in the Tetuan-Ceuta area, but admitted that he had been unable to penetrate inland where the secret fortifications were, and he received such a fright at the hands of the Spaniards that he refused further missions. We gave him 1000 francs a month just to sit in his shop and pick up news items, but after several months he refused the money, saying that he was not worth it. He was quite different from one of Mr. Strings' agents, who passed through the Spanish lines to his home in the Anjera and back at will.

Two other agents may be mentioned at this point; Mulay Ali and the Neanderthal. Mulay Ali was a leatherworker, from the tribe of Taghzuth in the Senhaja Sghir, an old friend of Browne's and an inveterate kif smoker. At Browne's bidding he came to Tangier, and made us many portfolios and pocketbooks as a cover job; meanwhile Browne sent him back and forth to Taghzuth on one excuse or another. He delivered certain information from his home area, and helped explode the Tamanrot airport myth. In these ways he was useful, but he had no idea of security, constantly broke cover, and was dangerous, so Browne paid him off and let him go.

The Neanderthal was a simple soul from the caves of Hercules, who had been my archaeological foreman in 1939 and a friend of Doolittle's. He lived near the caves and had a permit from the Spaniards to fish there. He came into town from time to time, selling us chickens, and told us the exact locations of Spanish troops between Sidi Kassem and Cap Spartel, and when these troops were changed. He also told us that the Spaniards had 2AA guns mounted on a truck sunk in the Phoenecian tomb, which permitted me to locate it within a few feet on a British aerial photograph obtained from Gibraltar, since I knew the Phoenecian tomb well from the time when I had been excavating with Dr. Nahon and Hooker Doolittle. He told us exactly what use the Spaniards were making of the caves, and kept us periodically informed of all Spanish activities in his area. I paid in return his property tax (tertib) and gave him a new jellaba. Later on he kept Browne informed of the movements of the German submarine which lay under the shelter of the Spanish AA guns over the caves, and which made occasional dashes out into the Straits to attack convoys. He was a most accurate and courageous informant, and his rustic simplicity and guilelessness served as good cover. At last knowledge he was still in the firm's employ.

One special intelligence job that Browne and I did during the last few days of June and early in July was to clock the road from Tangier to Melilla through the Spanish Zone, since we knew that if any military operations were to take place in that zone, the armies would have to make use of that road. We kept a log of the road on the speedometer, noting to a tenth of a kilometer the location of all cuts, banks, overhangs, culverts, and bridges; in other words, all targets either for demolition or air attack; at the same time we noted the position of all visible Spanish defenses. Later this log was turned over to Colonel Johnson, who sent it to G-2. A copy of it was in the hands of the Fifth Army in Oujda when I was working there in March and April of this year. A full report of this trip was handed to the State Department, but I will summarize some of the high points here.

The first day we went to Ktama. Along the way we were stopped every few miles by pairs of Guardia Civils in their George Washington hats, and they insisted on copying our passports. A number of them could not read or write, and had to hand the passports over to colleagues. In some instances we had to do the copying for them. One of them wrote down my name as Scar Right Thumb, a note which appears on my passport, but I corrected this for him, for he was very pleasant to us and I did not want him to get in trouble . . . they knew my name anyway. In some places they said, "O yes, you are Browne and Coon! Let us see your passports." No potentate's passage was more heralded than this one, no ambassador swept on with more pomp and courtesy.

Somewhere between Bab Taza and Ktama a soldier dashed out of a post and stopped us. Would we take the secret army mail on to Ktama? We would. We were handed a bundle of letters marked "Secret," and addressed to high commanding officers. It was a great temptation to open these and copy their contents, but since our passage was being clocked all the way, we had to arrive on time or plead a flat tire; furthermore, the envelopes were heavily sealed and we had no means to restore them if we should open them. So we simply handed them on when we arrived at Ktama, much to the consternation of the authorities, who undoubtedly thought we had read them.

At Ktama we met by chance a Lieutenant Colonel Sanchez Perez, who had been a captain in 1926–1927 at Suk et-Tnime of the Beni Amart; he and I and my wife were old friends, and since my Spanish was poor we conversed in Arabic, much to the colonel's delight, for it gave him a chance to show off before the other Spaniards present. We opened a bottle of 1847 sherry which I had brought from Gibraltar, and much friendship was enjoyed by all. He was the chief interventor of all the country from the River Nekor to Sheshawen, and since he is sympathetic with the natives, I believe he was an admirable choice. If all Spaniards were like him there would be little trouble in northern Morocco.

On the way up we stopped to take photographs of a much mooted spot, the alleged airport of Tamanrot a few miles west of Ktama. We had heard a lot about this from the British, who had even sent airplanes over to photograph it. We photographed it from the road and studied it with field glasses; at length we satisfied ourselves that there was no airport there, and confirmed this from a native merchant who had a shop there, and to whom, on the way back, we gave a ride as far as Sheshawen. In Ktama there was some secret at Suk et Tlata of Ktama, a few miles south of the hotel; when we tried to drive down there armed guards leaped out of the forest and stopped us. Later we found, from both Mulay Ali and Tassels, that there was nothing there but a few anti-aircraft batteries covering the airfield of Llano Amarillo, in front of the hotel. Thus we laid the ghosts of two alleged airports, which had bothered both G-2 and the British.

The second day we went from Ktama to Ajdir, and slept at Villa Sanjorjo; the third day we proceeded over the toboggan* to Beni Tuzin. In the afternoon we tried to visit the Suk es Sebt of Beni Tyeb in Beni Ulishk; it was Saturday and market day.

As we approached the town of Beni Tyeb, a Guardia Civil leaped over a hedge and stopped us. He was shivering and sweating, and he said, "I am ordered to stop you." I said, "We merely want to visit the market. Which is the road?"

"Yes, I know, but that is exactly where you *cannot* go."

"Why not?"

"Because we have a secret military camp there which we cannot let you see!"

"Where is it?"

"That is the trouble, it is *directly* in front of the market."

"Who is there?"

"Such and such and such and such; I lament it much (*Yo lamentolo mucho*), but now you see why I have orders not to let you go there."

We thanked this polite person very much, and proceeded on our way, pulling out the notebook after we were out of his line of vision. We proceeded to Melilla.

Here we called on Richard Croker, the British vice-consul, who was expecting us. The poor man had been in coventry for over a year; no Spaniard would speak to him. He was all alone. Hence he was very pleased to have two companions. He was tolerated because he had the power of giving navicerts for vessels taking ore out of the port; the British provided the Spanish with coal in return for ore. Yet he was hated. We spent the evening and the next day, the Fourth of July, with him. The following day the Afrika

---

* A very vulnerable and picturesque mountain road consisting of some thirty-odd hairpin turns.

Korps broke through to el Alamein, and almost to Alexandria. We went aboard a British vessel in the harbor. The captain kept the steam up, because it was a logical premise that if the Germans took Alexandria the Spaniards would march on Oujda and Oran. Croker was ready to hop on the ship, the captain to dash out of the harbor. About noon Browne and I got in our car and made tracks for Tangier. We may have been alarmists, but if the Germans had taken Alexandria we would have been trapped, and we were taking no unnecessary chances.

We arrived at Ktama late that night and left early the next morning, taking with us as a passenger Pepe de Hervas, a Spanish engineer who is the son-in-law of Mr. Dempster, a British employee of our Legation at Tangier. All went well until we came to the junction of the Tangier-Tetuan road. Here three men on a motorcycle and sidecar stopped us. They demanded the right to "enregistrar" our car. We thought that this meant to write down the number, which seemed a reasonable request, so we told them to go ahead, although Pepe told us not to let them. We soon saw that Pepe was right, for they proceeded to take out all the baggage and prod the cushions.

We then told them to stop, that this was a diplomatic vehicle and they had no right to search it. They said that they had specific orders to search this very vehicle and that if they failed to carry out their orders they would get in trouble. We told them that much as we regretted getting them in trouble, they could not do it. They were polite but very firm. We were the same. Finally one of them picked up Browne's portable radio receiving set, and started to walk off with it. I ran after him and took it away from him. Meanwhile Pepe was engaging in a heated conversation in rapid Spanish which I could not follow.

Finally they placed one of their men in our car and told us to follow them to Tetuan. They led us at a rapid pace, with their siren open, and to follow them we were forced to skid around corners on two wheels. Finally they drew up in front of the police station, and asked us to come in with them. I did so, and Pepe likewise, but Browne refused, stating that he would guard the car. Inside much palaver went on, which seemed to get us all nowhere. Pepe then disappeared, to see the chief interventor of Tetuan. Meanwhile, since we were parked in front of a café, and we were very hot and thirsty, Browne and I ordered beer for ourselves and the policemen. A number of them came out of the police station, and drank it with us. Everyone was in good spirits, and most of the police were apologetic.

Pepe returned, and we were allowed to proceed, under guard, to their chief interventor's office. He greeted us cordially and apologized. He said that a report had come in from some place to the east that we were carrying and operating a secret transmitting set, and that the police had had instructions to confiscate it. Of course, this was ridiculous, he said; we as accredited diplomats would do no such thing. We told him that we had a commercial receiving set, and that this was within our rights; furthermore, that although he had no right to have us searched, now that he had apologized and the affair was finished, we would be glad to show him the set just to satisfy his curiosity. He declined, rather wistfully.

It may be said concluding this section that although our primary concern was operations, this work necessarily involved what could be classifed as SI activities. We turned over suitable information to G-2 and to the State Department, and exchanged notes with the British. After Booth arrived, we turned over all non-operational intelligence to him. The two organizations, those of Tassels and Mr. Strings, gave us a constant supply of data that could not be obtained elsewhere. In my opinion it is impossible to divorce operations from intelligence since the former activity necessarily involves the latter. Furthermore, SO men are often in a better position, through their dealing with subversive groups, to

obtain information than are agents whose activities are by defini-
tion confined to intelligence.

TRAINING AND SMUGGLING

BEFORE coming to North Africa, Browne had had no training in
demolition, and I had had but ten days intensive work in Canada.
He needed some schooling, and I could do with a refresher. So
first he went to Gibraltar to study under that expert, Captain
Charles MacIntosh, and I followed. There we spent our time with
the Villa Lourdes crowd (the British SOE outfit), and with the
Independent Company, and our days spent with these men were
extremely happy ones. Not only was the work interesting, but our
companions were full of fun and among the finest of human
beings. At the Villa Lourdes one could expect to have a piece of
detonating cord go off under one's chair while drinking a glass of
beer; there were swimming bouts at Sandy Bay, and dinners with
Free Norwegian sailors aboard ML boats. I assisted MacIntosh in
his early researches into directional firing with plastic, which led
to the invention of the beehive. And it was there that we first got
the incentive to invent the Coon-Browne explosive turds.

At the request of SOE, Browne and I made a trip in July
through French Morocco to pick up typical stones along the
roads, so that the London office could dress up tire-bursters in
plaster of Paris to lay innocently along the roads to be traversed by
enemy vehicles. On this trip, which was difficult to arrange at a
time when gasoline was scarce, we discovered that there were very
few stones along the roads, but that mule turds were to be found
in great abundance. So to our stone collecting, which filled the
back seat, we added a few samples of local mule dung, and this
was carefully packed and sent to London. We took care to explain
that the full, rich horse dung of the British countryside would not
do in Morocco; it was the more watery, smaller-bunned mule type

that would pass there without suspicion. Also, it was important to have it a deep sepia color, sometimes with greenish shades, the product of straw and grass, not of oats and hay. In due course of time the British London office made up explosive turds from these samples, and we used them to good effect later in Tunisia.

During late August, September, and early October, I became a commuter between Gibraltar and Tangier. My business was to load .45 pistols, ammunition, Sten guns, flares, and other useful objects into British diplomatic pouches, and see that they got to the British Legation, after which I had to shift them to our Legation and then tote them down to Casablanca in a US navy pouch. Browne also made some of these trips. My chief obstacle was the British foreign office. On several occasions I had the pouches loaded and at the last minute I had to reduce the weight by half, remove all pistols, etc., etc., and this increased the frequency of my visits and made them all the more conspicuous.

The trouble was that each time I took a load across to Tangier, the Foreign Office in London had to cable specific approval, otherwise Colonel Brian Clarke could not let me take them. The Foreign Office had a nasty habit of cabling permission and then revoking it by another cable at the last minute. Sometimes these cables arrived a few minutes late, but we were seldom that lucky.

After I had packed the pouches, they had to be taken to the civil administrator's office to be sealed. Then they were handed over to two or more husky sergeants or junior officers, very conspicuous in civilian clothes, who took them to the ship and watched them during the passage. I was supposed to have no connection with those pouches, once I had packed them; I was not supposed to see them again, or to pay any attention to them, until they had been delivered to the SOE office in the British Legation. At that point I had to shift them to other containers and get them inconspicuously to our naval attaché's office.

This attempt to disassociate me publicly from the pouches made it difficult for me to keep constant track of them. I would be taken to the ship in one car, and the pouches with their couriers in another. On one occasion they let me get aboard the *Mayne*, after which the couriers brought the pouches. Then when the ship was about to push off, another carful of officials arrived and yanked the pouches off. I could not protest without making myself conspicuous, nor could I get off the ship for the same reason.

When I arrived in Tangier empty-handed, I saw Colonel Eddy on the dock waiting for me, with a number of armed men in the crowd, as well as Gregory Abrines, one of our Legation employees, who had several thousand pesetas to use as bribes if necessary. The cable telling Colonel Eddy that I had come without the pouches had not arrived. Everyone was keyed up for the landing, and we were all very disappointed. Colonel Eddy then said, "Go back on the *Mayne* tomorrow, and come back with your shield or on it."

I took this literally and came back with the pouches, which despite regulations I did not let out of my sight from the moment I had packed them. At the last moment I had to unpack and repack twice, and before I left, my pockets were searched for hand grenades. This journey required a special trip of the *Mayne*, and I had my friend Captain MacIntosh as chief courier. On this trip Major Douglas, the owner of the *Mayne*, steered the ship, for MacIntosh's benefit, so close to the Spanish shore that soldiers on the rocks fired at us with rifles.

In the trouble I had getting the arms and munitions across, the British SOE personnel were not to blame. It was the British Foreign Office, in concert with Mr. Gascoyne, who were responsible. They were afraid of a repetition of the explosion on the dock of February 5, 1942, in which eight Britishers and a number of Arabs lost their lives. Despite all our precautions, I find it hard to see why the Germans did not see that something unusual was going on, and attribute our success as much to their stupidity as to our precautions.

The British would not let us take any hand grenades over,

either in the pouches or in our luggage, so Browne and I found another way of getting them. Mr. Strings had a considerable supply left over from the Spanish Civil War, and he offered to let us have them. The first delivery was made at 5:30 on a Sunday morning, after the last revelers had been tucked in their beds and before the first churchgoers had arisen. Even the Moslems were not up at this time.

Idris, the Strings legman, packed a load onto a mule, laying them in the sides of a shwari, or native double panier. Over them he put cloths, a tea tray, sugar, mint, and a tea box. He and a friend started up the mountain, for we were to meet at el Farhar in the courtyard. I was there with the Plymouth waiting for him. Idris was a bit late, but when he came he was perfectly composed, and shifted the grenades into the bundle carrier. I let him proceed before I drove the Plymouth away. It seems that at the foot of the hill, while crossing the Wedel Yahoud, a Spanish soldier had stopped him and asked what was in the shwari. Idris said, "Tea and sugar, both contraband; we are going to have a picnic on the mountain. Here is fifty pesetas; let us through." The Spaniard took the fifty pesetas and they came up the mountain.

We made numerous trips to Casablanca with all these things packed in State Department pouches, some for Casa and others for Oran, Algiers, and Tunis. Nobody stopped us or made any trouble, although we heard that the Germans had complained that we were passing hand grenades and offered a large reward for the name of the man who gave them to us. In Casa on one trip I instructed Dave King and Staff Reid in the use of the Sten gun, so that they could in turn teach their men, and so that when they took the other pouches on to Oran and Algiers they could give similar instruction. I was to have gone on a teaching trip as far as Tunis, but this was considered too conspicuous.

On our return trips we smuggled other commodities, such as flour and kuskus semolina for Mr. Strings and other Moorish friends, and champagne for European friends. On one return trip

Browne and Captain Holcomb smuggled in Malverne, the chief pilot of Port Lyautey, who was sent to Gib, London, and Washington and came in as pilot of the invasion fleet, but that is Browne's story and I will let him tell it. My own smuggling activities ended when I was sent to Gibraltar to take over communications and prepare for the eventuality of a landing at Ajdir to stir up the Riffians.

COMMUNICATIONS

WHEN I arrived in Tangier we had several techniques of communication. COINFORM (later changed to VICTOR) cabled us from Washington by a code which Colonel Eddy kept in the naval attaché's office safe, and which we worked in that office. OSS cables came addressed to Colonel Eddy, Naval Attaché, U.S. Legation, Tangier, although half the time they were erroneously labeled "Military Attaché." Then Browne and I had private codes, which we used little at first, but once when the office code was compromised for several weeks over a very critical period, all communications with Washington were carried on by means of my private code. I had a little difficulty with this code because of one word, "desiccated." At both ends we apparently spelled it some three or four ways, and until we got this straightened out a number of messages had to be repeated.

I will not soon forget the day when I was decoding a message from London in our office code, and found that some thirty letters had come through in the clear; these thirty letters not only told what we were up to, for they discussed the preparation of forged passports, but also gave away the code, since at each end the letters formed part of a longer word. When I discovered this I was so overcome with disgust that I cursed vigorously in a loud voice, which could be heard throughout the Legation, and consequently, had to make up a story to explain this reaction to the legitimate State Department people. This was when it became nec-

[*35*]

essary to use my desiccated code, until a new office code could be
sent us through Lisbon.

At the time of my arrival Colonel Eddy had already set up the
five secret radio stations of Tangier (Midway), Casablanca (Lincoln), Oran (Franklin), Algiers (Yankee), and Tunis (Pilgrim).
The STORK (Sergeant Joseph Cryan) was running Midway, Ajax
(a Frenchman) was running Lincoln, Frederick Brown (a Frenchman who cannot speak a word of English, despite his name) was
running Yankee, and I never knew who ran the other two. I did
not even know about Brown until after the landing; I never knew
Ajax's real name, and never saw him until March 1943. As with
all other phases of the TORCH operation, Colonel Eddy told no
one anything he did not need to know. I did not want to know
who these men were. Needless to say, none of the Snakepit (State
Department) people knew anything about our clandestine sets,
either in Tangier or elsewhere, except of course for Murphy and
Springs and John Boyd. Bob Murphy and John Boyd were running Yankee in Algiers, and Springs, who was both Snakepit and
OSS, was doing the same with Pilgrim in Tunis. Childs, Russell,
and Doolittle were all equally ignorant. This ignorance caused
some embarrassment and some conflict.

For example, when I arrived at Tangier, the Stork (our Tangier
operator) was installed in his nest on the Legation roof; Mrs.
Childs complained that the tapping of the key at night disturbed
her sleep, so Mr. Childs ordered the set removed from the Legation. It is idle to point out that the success of the invasion was
more important than Mrs. Childs's sleep; Mr. Childs would
surely have admitted that, had he known. We could not put up an
argument without spilling something and so we moved the set.

The Stork, therefore, moved his set to a small villa on the
mountain which Colonel Eddy rented from Mr. Sinclair, the retired governor-general of Zanzibar. Ishaq, the colonel's confidential chauffeur and tough-man, took the Stork there every morning

and brought him back to his digs every night. But someone had to sleep in the nest lest our friends the Krauts should walk in and smash or blow up the set during the night, and in fact the villa could not be left untenanted at any time. This task of sleeping with the set fell to Browne and myself. Colonel Eddy was in Washington at the time, and we took it upon ourselves to do this. At first we both slept there every night, but we got little sleep; every time Mr. Sinclair's mule would kick a bush we would leap up and stalk around the villa; since we had full-time jobs in the daytime, we were missing too much sleep, and therefore we took turns. Sleeping there alone was not very restful.

After a while Ishaq agreed to take turns with us, so we were able to sleep two out of three nights each instead of one out of two. On one occasion Ishaq awoke in a cold sweat of horror on the couch; some huge heavy creature was pinning his chest, and he opened his eyes to look into two huge, luminous widely spaced eyes a few inches from his own. When he got control of his muscles he reached up and tried to grab the creature by the throat; it, however, let out a bass squawk and hopped over his head to the floor—it was a huge, thirty-pound bullfrog.

Aside from these duties Ishaq fed the Stork his noonday meal, which Ishaq prepared on a charcoal stove in the kitchen. There was a small well-chosen library in the nest, and I remember, during my nights on watch, reading a two-volume work on the history of the Parsees. It was in this nest also that Browne and I occasionally had our meetings with Tassels.

Since Browne and I were sometimes called away on trips, to Melilla, to Casablanca, to Gibraltar, this guarding duty became increasingly onerous, and our absence from our rooms all night increasingly conspicuous. So we arranged with Stripes, our British colleague, to furnish a guard of Gibraltareans and Spanish Reds to sleep there every night. Ishaq had the duty of feeding these men, and they developed enormous appetites, particularly for red wine, so that we had to set ceilings on their consumption. Ishaq was particularly upset about the cost of this victualing; our chief concern was to keep the watchdogs sober.

Finally, a few weeks before D, we rigged a new W/T room on the roof of the naval attaché's office, further away from the scene of Mrs. Childs's slumbers than the old nest, and during the absence of the Childs family in Lisbon we put the Stork back where he belonged. When the Childses arrived in Tangier after a six-week rest, some few days before D, the restoration of the Stork was a fait accompli, and events of a far more shattering nature soon occurred to reduce the Stork affair into insignificance in the Childian mind.

About a month before D, Gordon Browne was sent to Gibraltar by Colonel Eddy to take over communications at that post; Colonel Eddy shifted the central office from Tangier to Gibraltar, keeping Tangier only as a listening post. About a week later I went over to relieve Gordon. Malcolm Henderson (British SIS man under the notorious Colonel Ellis) also went over. In Gib I found Gordon installed in a dank cubicle in the JIC office, deciphering the messages which came in every day from the outlying stations, and keeping the code keys in a black box furnished by the British.

This box had a British padlock on it, and it was conceivable to my mind that there might be more than one key, so I substituted a lock and key, of Swedish manufacture, which I had brought over from Tangier. At this time I also changed the codes, substituting new keys which Colonel Eddy and I made up and sent to the various posts, with instructions to put them in operation when so instructed. This was done not so much to prevent our British colleagues from cracking our messages as to confound the enemy in case they had broken down our old codes. The period of transition was somewhat painful, as messages came for several days in both old and new codes.

The system was that the messages would be received by the

British in their two stations in the Rock; Squadron Leader Mallory, whom we all called "Bombshell," had charge of these stations, and sent the messages down by dispatch rider to me at the JIC. I would decipher them, and file the messages in my black box. If any message required a decision, I had instructions to confer with Colonel Brian Clark, Coldstream Guards, and local head of the SOE under Colonel Eddy. However, I had the right to make decisions pending the arrival of Colonel Eddy.

Gordon was only too pleased to relinquish this task to me; he was very tired. Furthermore, a mysterious Lieutenant Marachi, US Signal Corps, had arrived from London with a mysterious secret weapon; this was "Rebecca," the signaling device by which Browne was to bring parachute planes into a spot between Tafaroui and La Senia, the airfields of Oran, on D night. Lieutenant Marachi had been ordered to instruct Browne in the use of this device. Lieutenant Colonel Henderson, however, also wanted to be instructed; he said that London (presumably SIS) had given him orders to learn also. Marachi, however, had had no orders to instruct Henderson, and a pretty dilemma ensued; it looked like another attempt on the part of SIS to penetrate the activities of OSS-SOE, and Browne, Brian Clarke, Marachi, and I held long conferences on this subject. Finally we decided to let Marachi instruct Henderson, on the basis that he was a right guy and our friend; we took a personal rather than an institutional line. Henderson never went to Oran, and we never did find out exactly how this confusion had arisen.

Marachi, Browne, and Henderson took Rebecca into the governor's palace and the instruction took place on the governor's living-room floor. Once he had learned his lesson Browne took Rebecca over to Tangier in a diplomatic pouch and eventually proceeded with it to Oran. What happened there is Browne's story and I will let him tell it; all I need say here, in case he omits it, is that his courageous action has been appreciated in the proper quarters and, the last time I was in Algiers, Colonel Tarr of the

U.S. Air Force told me that he was going to see that Browne got a Silver Star for it.

As the messages poured in with increasing frequency every day, I grew more and more fatigued. I had a single room in the Rock Hotel, although brigadiers were heaped up three to a room. General Eisenhower arrived under the name of General Howe, which fooled nobody since some soldiers brought his baggage, marked "Lt. Gen. Dwight D. Eisenhower," publicly through the streets of Gibraltar. General Clark was General Mark, and the presence of his black orderly did not make his identity difficult. General Doolittle arrived and Colonel Harold Willis dashed up and down the length of Gibraltar in his jeep, which he had brought from England in a Douglas transport. The great were convening; Olympus was crowded with gods; the Lords of the East and of the West, of the Air, Land, and Sea; it made me think of Housman's lines: "The king with half the East at heel is marched from lands of morning; Their fighters drink the rivers up, their shafts benight the air," and why the enemy did not correctly read these omens and foresee the greatest amphibious operation since Xerxes crossed the Hellespont, none of us could see.

Furthermore, if the enemy had drawn up a graph of daily frequency of messages from our stations, they would have seen the line mounting swiftly, day by day, at almost a 45-degree angle; soon Yankee was on the air all the time, and the others most of it.

The work was too much for me to handle alone. Haley Morris, Bombshell Mallory, Sergeant Potter (one of the DRs), and another DR whom we knew only as Yorkshire, and even Brian Clark himself rolled up their sleeves while the rain slogged down outside the door, and helped me with the double transposition. I alone made out the keys; I was under orders to let no Britisher have the code, and although this sometimes held things up a little, I followed my orders. My cubicle in the JIC was an island of American nationality.

Even blocking out the keys grew to be too much for me, since the messages were coming in twenty-four hours a day and I was getting but one- and two-hour snatches of sleep. So I got in touch with two other Americans, Ensign Kitts of the Naval Observer's office, and Captain Connors of the Signal Corps, and taught them the keys. With their help I got a little more rest, but not much. Then, at about D-8, Colonel Eddy sent Chief Yeoman Peter Hetzler over from Tangier to help me, and at about D-5 he came over himself.

Colonel Eddy's arrival was a great relief. I had been handling the lengthy and complicated messages from Bob Murphy concerning his conversations with Giraud, and when Giraud wanted the landing put off two weeks, Brian Clark and I said *no* very emphatically. We knew that the armada was already at sea and no delay could be made.

When Colonel Eddy arrived I was able to put my files in order; I had been working at such a tempo that I had simply thrown the messages in the box; now under Eddy's direction it was possible to bring some order into this tangle. Also, he was there to make the decisions.

His departure from Tangier required considerable planning not to give the show away. He kept his rooms in the Minza, and left most of his clothing there; he told them that he would be gone a few days. Previously I had kept my room and left my clothes in it. Even the number of trips of the *Mayne* had to be kept down to an apparently normal number; we could not put on too many extra voyages lest this tip our hand to the enemy.

During the last few days we turned more and more over to the British. We gave Bombshell our Yankee code, and this relieved us of nearly half the burden of enciphering and deciphering. Later we gave them all the codes.

I will never forget sending out to all stations the warning to listen for the message over the French-language BBC to be broadcast early in the evening of November 7—"*Ecoute, Yankee* [Franklin, Lincoln, Pilgrim, in each case] *Robert arrive, Robert*

arrive," or *"Robert arrive trois heures en retard,* etcetera." We
had to have confirmation that this message had been received,
and the Franklin confirmation arrived dangerously late.

On the fateful night Eddy, Hetzler, Kitts, and I repaired to
Commander O'Brien's office in the consulate, where we sat up
with him and with Lieutenant Colonel Carl Holcomb, the military observer, who was in his pajamas, not knowing that anything
was to happen. We ate ham sandwiches and drank beer, and soon
came the historic broadcast in several languages: I remember most
clearly the German: *"Achtung—achtung—achtung—Meldun-
gen von den Vereinten Staten von Amerika—Achtung, achtung,
achtung. Ein amerikanisches kraftsheer ist auf den nordwest
Kuste Afrikas gelandet; ein amerikanisches kraftsheer is auf den
nordwest Kuste Afrikas gelandet*—and then, Franklin Roosevelt
in his Grotonian French, making his announcement to the
French people. Then the *Marseillaise* and the *Star Spangled Ban-
ner.* Eddy and I, groggy with excitement and lack of sleep, went
back to the office and made out a message to General Donovan.
And then we slept.

CHAPTER THREE

First Interim

Historical Setting: November and December 1942

ALL the landings were successful, those at Casablanca and Algiers running into little significant resistance. At Oran, however, General Auguste Nogues put up a stiff, prolonged fight, giving a taste of what might have happened, and might still happen in other places. After several days Nogues yielded to political and military pressures.

After the landings, the working conditions of OSS members changed considerably. Now they were in direct contact with the military in the field, sometimes involved in formal actions, and they frequently found their functions misunderstood by commanders who wanted to use them as some form of combat infantry. This was a complaint heard from special forces, American and British alike, throughout the war in all theaters. As Coon indicates, when OSS people had to work closely with the army, they were usually best off if they could set up a partnership with Counter Intelligence.

While the status quo continued in Tangier and the Spanish Zone of Morocco, in French North Africa the political problems sharpened. The State Department, which continued to maintain an ambassador in Madrid and had kept one also in Vichy, put all its faith in the existing hierarchy of Vichy-affiliated officials still in authority in the French-controlled territories. It was not enthusiastic about stirring up native anti-German activity that would also be anticolonial. Robert Murphy, the leading Allied conspirator in French North Africa who unsuccessfully championed General Henri Giraud as his candidate, also believed that only the colonial French could be effective against the Germans and wanted all OSS funds and assistance channeled to them. As if to complicate matters more, Colonel Robert Solborg, an OSS official to whom Coon refers early in his narrative, also went to North Africa and without orders, to back a French candidate of his own, and soon faded from the scene.

Whatever the American Army and General Eisenhower may have felt about French versus native support and keeping the Vichy governments in power, they argued military necessity. In truth, the forces put ashore were dangerously small for their fighting job, let alone administrative and police functions. Although not supported by Robert Murphy, the most powerful Vichy figure then in Africa was Admiral Jean-Louis Darlan. He offered a cessation of fire by French forces, plus cooperation against the Germans, in exchange for recognition as the legitimate governing authority in French North Africa. Eisenhower took the deal, and defended his action vigorously against the howls of outrage in England and the United States by anticolonialists and pro–Free French, who weren't necessarily the same people.

The OSS view was that native support was essential and that money and effort be devoted to the various kinds of Arabs and Berbers among whom the military and most of the diplomats could not differentiate. Failure to do at least this, as Coon points out in a different connection, made a double-edged sword out of Roosevelt's extremely popular Four Freedoms speech. The OSS perceived that the French would not last long in Africa without war conditions to support them, so it stayed within its mandate keeping lines open as well as possible to all parties.

During the frantic period just before the landings, Coon shows displeasure with and suspicion of one branch of the British SIS (Secret Intelligence Service). That branch was manned by "sleepers," men who spend the best parts of their lives in sensitive places (e.g., Tangier), and develop a strong sense of territoriality when their nest grows hot and other agents in both intelligence and operations invade their private territories. There is a bit more of this later on, and it represents, especially in this case, an antagonism between Operations and Intelligence that has existed ever since there have been secret services. The attitude of Intelligence, somewhat simplified, is that Operations is a disturbing factor. Intelligence does most of its work by establishing agents in place and slowly building networks that are fragile creations. A guiding principle has been not to use information if its use discloses its source or tells the enemy that he has been penetrated. Operations, according to Intelligence, dislocates or destroys the valuable results of years of work with its explosions and assassinations, often at the cost of friendly lives. Furthermore, by arbitrarily and often blindly altering circumstances, Operations sets in train unknowable consequences.

In Tangier both the British SOE (Special Operations Executive) and the SO (Special Operations branch of the OSS) were natural, indeed inevitable, targets for agents of the SIS. That they should share this hostility in roughly equal measure was natural enough, for William Donovan modeled the OSS in considerable part on the SOE, begun some two years previously, and many OSS men were British trained. Donovan's counterpart, General Colin Gubbins, in his turn had borrowed substantially from his old antagonist, the Irish Republican Army, in developing his formidable SOE. (General Gubbins receives a somewhat more detailed introduction when he appears later in person. It should also be noted that Captain Gubbins, frequently mentioned in connection with Cap Serrat and the other outposts, is indeed the general's son.)

Colonel William A. Eddy, who becomes especially important to the narrative about the time of the landings, was a man of extraordinary ability combined with personal qualities that completely commanded Coon's loyalty and affection. Eddy's professional reputation was deservedly prodigious, although he was hard to classify. He served both the OSS and the State Department at various times. His military rank, although in a sense a cover, was real, well earned, and acquired in a normal way. Grandson of the founder of the American University of Beirut, born in Sidon of a missionary family, Eddy was a student at Princeton at the beginning of World War I. He joined the Marine Corps, was wounded in France, and decorated for bravery in action. When peace came, he took up teaching in Egypt and then for a number of years was president of Hobart College in upper New York State. He rejoined the marines during World War II. After the events Coon recounts, Eddy was named minister plenipotentiary to Saudi Arabia and went to live in Jidda, the port of Mekka. From there, in 1945, he was the man who made possible the almost unbelievable voyage of the old, crippled King Ibn Sa'ud on the American destroyer Murphy to a meeting with president Roosevelt on the Great Bitter Lake in the Suez Canal.

When Eddy moved OSS headquarters to Algiers in late 1942, he was following the rapid eastward movement of events made possible by Eisenhower's agreement with Admiral Darlan. Darlan's authority coincided, not surprisingly, with the range of the Allied landings, covering the immense stretch of territory from Casablanca on the Atlantic to Oran and Algiers on the Mediterranean. In that area he saved Eisenhower any further active or passive military resistance, eased his long lines of communications, and reduced the danger of attack from Spanish territory, at least to a certain extent. All this was of great value, but it cost a price, administrative and police control being left in Darlan's hands, and the acceptance of Darlan himself.

Politically, Darlan was a very hot potato, hotter than Eisenhower imagined. Man of Vichy, cynic, pictured everywhere as even worse than he was, affiliation with him did serious damage to America's reputation in Africa and throughout the world. The British, able to wash their hands of Darlan and yet to profit from him, did both, making virtuous sounds about their support of de Gaulle, with whom they were actually quite unhappy, nor was Franklin Roosevelt pleased with Murphy's inability to replace Darlan with Giraud.

Darlan's writ did not run as far as Tunis, the port city of Tunisia which Vichy had allowed the Axis to use as a supply base, along with the harbor of Bizerta, for all their North African operations. In Tunis the French commander Admiral Jean-Pierre Esteva cooperated with the Germans. With 5000 Axis troops there from the beginning, supported by numerous second- and third-generation Italian colonials, it would have been difficult for Esteva to have done otherwise had he wished. And there were soon a great many more Germans. Tunis had to be fought for.

After Coon's move to OSS headquarters in Algiers, he is sketchy about his doings during the grim days surrounding Christmas in 1942, and understandably so. On December 24 he drove through Algiers on his way to the British Massingham mess at Cap Matifou, where he was staying as an instructor of the de Gaullist Free Corps of Africa. Held up by traffic in the midtown streets, he skirted the jam only dimly aware that he was circumnavigating Darlan's assassination. Soon after he reached Massingham, a French officer hurried in and announced that Darlan had been killed. He added that the killer was Fernand Bonnier de la Chapelle, a twenty-year-old student of Coon's in the basic special forces curriculum of communications, explosives, and weapons.

Somewhat curiously, de la Chapelle was a royalist, but that did not prevent the authorities from rounding up numbers of Free French and many others whom they wished to harass. No one knew in which directions or how far a reign of terror might go. As

Coon relates it, Captain Sabattier, head of the camp at Ain Taya where Coon did his teaching, was arrested, and so were several instructors who worked for Coon. For the sake of others as well as himself, it seemed a good idea for Coon to drop out of sight. Doing so led first to the adventure of his lapsed papers, then his trip to Guelma with Eddy, and his assignment to the outpost of Cap Serrat in Tunisia.

The Death of Darlan

I do not find it particularly agreeable to look back on the period from November 8 to December 31, 1942. It was a messy, chopped-up period of transition, and in fact, I find it hard to remember the order of my activities during this interval. Little of importance either to the war effort or to me happened as far as my personal activities were concerned, and I shall try to get over this period as quickly as possible.

For the next several days Colonel Eddy and I remained in Gib, tapering off the messages. I worried a little about Gordon Browne, from whom we had not heard, and continually framed tentative messages to his wife, Eleanor. When word finally came through that he was all right it was a considerable relief, and we soon had the appropriate message under way.

I did not know what I was to do next. Colonel Eddy was ordered to Algiers but I was not; so I went back to Tangier, which seemed a terrific letdown. For the next ten days I wanted to rest, but two affairs interrupted me. They were the Sheshawen Parachutists and the Carlos affair.

On the morning of November 8, a Douglas paratroop plane landed at Tentuan. Lieutenant Litsey, the pilot, got out and asked the Spaniards at the airport for gasoline, since he intended to refuel and go on to Oran. The Spaniards ordered all the parachutists out, disarmed them, and trotted them off to barracks. They kept them six days, and on the seventh they took them up to She-shawen.

The following day I went to Sheshawen to represent Mr. Childs and see what could be done for them. Since there were also RAF personnel interned there, I took Pepe Imossi, of the British Consulate at Tetuan, with me. This was just as well, because I could not speak Spanish well enough for the task involved. On the other hand, it was somewhat unfortunate because once we met the parachutists Pepe insisted on doing all the talking, and in giving the boys rather puerile boarding-school pep talks in a *Tom Brown's School Days*–style.

We went first to the Spanish Commandancia, and saw the commandante in charge. He was a tiny blond man who seemed greatly perturbed. He talked at great length, explaining how he was doing all he could to help the boys and how it was all very difficult and unfortunate. He detailed all the things he had done for them, so that we would have a pro-Spanish outlook when we should meet them. When we did, we could well understand his reason.

We found that the Spaniards had put the officers in the town hotel, with the British officers; the American enlisted men were in a Spanish barracks some distance away. Whereas the officers had the run of the town, the men could only visit the neighboring park and a few adjacent streets. While in the park they had attempted to play baseball, but a miniature Spaniard had come up, grabbed the arm of one of them, and said no! Then they had tried to play cards in the park, and someone else had said no! They did not realize that their offense lay not in playing ball or cards, but in doing it in the park. Not one of the Americans could speak Spanish nor could any of the Spanish speak English. Nor could any combination of Americans and Spaniards be found in which both spoke French. So the two groups were completely isolated linguistically.

The officers were angry at the Spaniards for separating them from their men; the men were very angry because they had been all steamed up to fight at Oran and now were stuck in what they considered a jail. They were screaming and shouting and one private walked around and around repeating "Fuck! Fuck!" with the regularity of a Tibetan lama repeating his "Om Mane Padme Hum," and banging his fist against the wall. They were all upset, and Pepe's Oxford accent and Wodehousean vocabulary infuriated them. They kept taking me aside and asking, "Who the hell is that Limey?"

The Spanish commandante came in with us and the paratroopers would go up to him one at a time and shout down on his head, which barely reached their shoulders; he in turn would shrug his shoulders, wave his hands, and shout at Pepe. Finally I succeeded in convincing the men that they should be quiet, and that we would do all we could for them.

They wanted to make a break and run for the French border. They had each a roll of plastic with them. They had worn this at the time of their landing in belts around their waists. When the Spaniards disarmed them they tasted this, thinking it candy. One Spaniard spit it out, and then they gave it back to the paratroopers, who still had it, but they had no detonators or fuses. I convinced them to delay this break, on the grounds that it would plunge the United States into war with Spain and deflect several divisions of our troops from the Tunisian front, thus delaying operations.

They would not be satisfied with a long delay, however, and I said that we would arrange some escape plan if they did not get out in a reasonable time. Later, on December 8, when two of them were in Tangier to have their teeth attended to, we laid on a plan with the help of Mr. Strings, which might well have worked.

Pepe and I managed to make an agreement between Lieutenant Litsey and the commandante permitting the men to go to the movies, eat in restaurants, play ball outside the barracks, etcetera, which satisfied them for the moment. I had brought some cigarettes and chocolate, and gave the officers some snap-knives. When I got back to Tangier, Mr. Childs made plans to furnish them with blankets, warm clothing, food, writing paper, games, and the like. Mrs. Winterbottom, a public-minded lady from Boston who lives in Tangier, took charge of the collection of goods for the boys, and subsequently someone from the Legation visited them at least once a week until the time of their release.

Three other planes landed at Imezoren airport in the Riffian tribe of Beni Urriaghel. This caused us some uneasy moments, for in our Tassels plan paratroops were to have landed there that night. Fortunately the first signals (two white flares dropped from a plane the night before) had not been given, and the Riffians had enough sense not to rush the Spaniards. But they might well have taken this visitation as a part of the plan and started a revolt which would have altered the course of that part of the war. The fifty-three paratroopers who landed at Imezoren were interned at Taounia outside Melilla. Our representatives visited them periodically also, although it was a long haul from Tangier. One of the captains interned at Taouina told me later at Oujda that a whole company of the Spanish Army there offered to take him and his men across the border if he would guarantee them enlistment in the American Army.

It is easy to see why the presence of these paratroopers caused the Spaniards discomfort. The Americans were about twice as big as the Spaniards, and had to have much better food. They slept on cots which the Spaniards brought up from Tetuan, while the Spanish soldiers slept on the floor. They had good uniforms while the Spaniards were in rags. Both the Spanish soldiers and the natives, military and civilian alike, could make the obvious comparison, and it was the best pro-American and anti-Franco propaganda in the world just to have those boys on view. Hence it was not long before the Spanish government found some pretext to remove them to Madrid and thence send them overland to Gibraltar.

The Carlos affair started as soon as I reached Tangier from Gibraltar, and took most of my time in Tangier. It seems that while we were at Gibraltar a Spanish Red named Carlos approached David Williamson, who had arrived in Tangier shortly before D day, to take over SI work. Carlos told Williamson that he was working for Colonel Eddy. He also said that all of his gang except himself had been arrested and probably shot, and that he needed to be hidden. So Dave hid him in the house of Mrs. Thomas. Now Betty Thomas had told Colonel Eddy that she would not mind using her house as a safe house for one-night jobs. But she did not want it used for long periods.

When I arrived she called me up, and I went to see her. It seems that Carlos had been there for two weeks, and was getting on her nerves. He sat in a spare bedroom on the ground floor all the time, smoking cigarettes and reading cheap Spanish translations of Edgar Wallace. Every day his girlfriend came to visit him. She was supposed to bring him news, but she was probably there for more personal administrations, for like all other Spanish agents of my acquaintance Carlos required frequent feminine attention.

I told Mrs. Thomas that I would try to find another place for Carlos, and would get him out as soon as I could. Dave Williamson turned over to me the entire Carlos affair. This business of finding a hideout was not easy, and I tried several prospects without success. Then finally Mr. Strings agreed to hide him, and Gusus and I rehearsed the delivery. I did not like it because I did not believe that mixing Spaniards and Moslems would work, and I did not want to burn Mr. Strings, but the only other alternative was killing Carlos, which I was not prepared to do at that point.

I was going to shift him after dark on Saturday night, but that afternoon Mrs. Thomas called me up in considerable agitation. When I arrived she explained that she had seen three Spanish policemen searching her lawn, and she asked them what they were doing. They replied that they were looking for some boys who had been throwing stones onto the tin roof of Miss Greene, a neighbor.

They poked around her shrubbery, and walked up on the steps; she went in and warned Carlos. He ran out of the back door with his suitcase. One of the police saw him ducking around the bushes, and they set forth in hot pursuit, but Carlos ducked around some more shrubbery and disappeared. Then they asked Miss Greene's Moorish gardener which way the man had gone, and the gardener misdirected them. He did this not because he knew Carlos or had any interest in the affair, but simply because he was a Moor and they the Spanish police. No Moor would ever give them any aid if he had any choice in the matter.

Mrs. Thomas was sure that her house was burned, and was afraid that Carlos would return if he was not captured. I agreed to keep in constant touch with her. Later I went to the Legation, and Alexander, Mr. Childs's chauffeur, who without Mr. Childs's knowledge acted as go-between for us with the Spanish Reds, came to tell me that Carlos was hiding in the so-called British Garage. How he ever got from Mrs. Thomas's shrubbery to the other side of town without detection is still a mystery.

I put him in my car under some gasoline tins and drove him up to the Mountain, where I lodged him in Colonel Eddy's villa. Then I went down to see Kirby Greene who lived a mile or so lower down. Coe Greene had a good laugh, because the Spanish police really were looking for boys throwing stones. Coe had put in the complaint himself on behalf of his sister. The Spanish police had not in all probability identified Carlos in any way with Mrs. Thomas. Coe agreed to hide out Carlos in the morning.

I then returned to the villa and slept there with Carlos, keeping guard. In the morning I draped him under the gasoline tins again and picked up Coe Greene, and we went, by a roundabout way, to a house owned by the proprietor of the Sphinx Restaurant and Sphinx Bar. The man who owned it was a French de Gaullist; he worked in the garage and his wife in the bar. We drove under the house and let Carlos out. He had strict instructions not to leave the house under any circumstance unless so instructed by us.

Two days later the Frenchman sent word that he wanted to see me. I arranged a meeting in Ishaq's house. Mr. and Mrs. Frenchman were there. Mme. was weeping, Mr. was angry. They were both out for blood. It seems that Carlos had gone out without permission. Then a Spaniard had come while the two (Mr. and Mrs.) were out, as well as Carlos. He had rung the bell of the flat below by mistake, apologized, and flashed a badge. Then he went upstairs and unlocked the French door, and ransacked the house, removing two sporting rifles belonging to Mr. Frenchman. Carlos had not returned.

Mr. and Mrs. Frenchman claimed that Carlos was a Franco agent planted there to burn them. They claimed the rifler had taken the shotguns for identification, that Mr. Frenchman belonged to some club *sportif de chasse,* and that his guns were well known. He could not go hunting because he had no gun, and this would cause wide comment; he could not report the loss of the gun. They were *foutus.* It was all my fault.

Shortly after that I had the good fortune to leave Tangier, and to dump this problem on Browne. The upshot was that the Frenchman hid out in Buckingham's for several months, in fact most of the winter, while his wife went to Casa, and they lost their house. Carlos had not been a fascist plant. The fascists had taken him to Tetuan, where they tortured him, and then to Spain, where they shot him.

Before Thanksgiving I went to Casablanca, and lived about a week with Dave King in his house. I was very tired and jumpy, and so was he. At the end of this week Vice-Consul Harry Blank and I made a trip to Fez for General Keyes and Colonel (now General) Wilbur. Our purpose was to determine the exact way in which the French distributed food and clothing materials to the natives, the exact system of taxing natives, and the methods of controlling native circulation and transport. We spent several days in Fez obtaining detailed information from seven prominent natives, all of whom we persuaded to talk freely. When we returned we handed our report in, and Colonel Wilbur, after reading it, exclaimed: "Why, that is exactly the Nazi system of exploitation." Then he asked, "How long has this been going on?" "Twenty years," I replied. Then he said, "Too long for us to do anything about it at this point." General Patton made it clear to me that we did not have the men to police North Africa; that we had, through this paucity of numbers, to leave the French in complete control of the natives however unjustly they might be treating them; and that our job was simply to kick the Axis out of North Africa with the men at our disposal. I told him that this policy might boomerang, that the natives might be aroused against us to such an extent that it might impede our military operations, but his point was clear; he had his instructions and the North African campaign was being waged with a dangerously small number of soldiers.

Several disquieting things happened during the period. Just before the Americans entered Marrakesh the French officials quietly bought up all the tea and sugar from the native shops; later, when the Americans had come, they stated that the Americans had cleaned these vital commodities out of the town. They would stop at nothing to discredit us with the natives and prevent the natives from developing close and friendly relations with us. They were and still are mortally afraid that we will establish ourselves with the natives.

Our failure to take relations with the natives seriously enough had an appreciable military effect in one area at one time—in the Tebessa-Kasserine area during the February withdrawal. Then and later in the two-corps area the Arabs helped the Germans against us, and their help was of considerable strategic value to the enemy. However, in Morocco, the results of our policy, while disquieting, had had no military effect up to the time of the taking of Tunis on May 8; and now it is presumably too late.

Now that North Africa is quiet I hope that we can repair these omissions, if only to keep in some measure our word as a nation as expressed in the declaration of the Four Freedoms. As we proceed in the capture of Axis-held territory we must keep our word in this respect, or we will find the Axis-conquered peoples, as we go further, helping not us but the Axis, or at least indifferent in their work against the Axis behind the lines. Our policy of liberation is our strongest weapon, and it rusts more quickly than steel and deteriorates more rapidly than explosives.

Upon my return from Fez, I went to Algiers with Dave King to consult with Colonel Eddy. We were both uncertain about our activities in the immediate future. In Algiers I contracted a bad cold which later turned out to be pneumonia. We had a gathering of the Torch gang at that point, with Rounds, Knight, Springs, King, and myself all present. At this time I met Colonel Keswick and Major Gillis of the Massingham mission, and this meeting led to my association with their group in the near future.

Leland Rounds was also ill, and we occupied adjoining beds in the Aletti. My bed was without a blanket, but I finally bribed an Arab servant to loan me a rug. After two nights in that bed I went back to Casablanca; King stayed longer. Colonel Eddy had secured for me a seat on General Clark's private plane, which was going to Oujda. From there I would find my own way to Casablanca. Things were that way with air transport in those days; a passenger argued his way onto a plane only to be dumped off at Tafaroui or some other place to have to argue his way onto another plane. No regular system of handling passenger traffic had yet been devised.

When I got up in the dark on the morning of my departure, I saw a group of generals and colonels in the hall of the Aletti, and we paid our bills together. I had a Buick all to myself and offered to take some of them with me to the airport, but they declined. I assumed that this was General Clark's group, and when we reached the Maison Blanche airport I therefore got on the same plane that they entered. This was a luxurious Douglas transport fitted with velvet seats, instead of the aluminum bucket seats to which I had grown accustomed. Besides a number of colonels, I saw three brigadier generals, whom I later identified as General Fitzgerald, Grant, and Smith. I did not see General Clark, but assumed that he would soon appear.

As I discovered soon after, this was a group of officers of the West African Ferry Command up from Accra to inspect North African airports, and the plane was General Fitzgerald's private carrier. A brigadier whom I later identified as General Fitzgerald turned to me after I had taken a seat and said: "What the hell are you doing on my plane?"

"I am on my way to Casa," I said. "General Clark told me that he would take me with him as far as Oujda."

"Well, you are on the wrong plane and get the hell off. This is not General Clark's plane; I am General Fitzgerald and it is my plane."

"Where are you going?" I asked.

"Casa," he said.

"Then," I said, "if you do have room and can take me, would you mind letting me stay here? I have to get to Casa at once and General Clark is only going to Oujda."

I thought that General Fitzgerald would burst a few blood vessels at this point. We argued for a few moments, until finally General Fitzgerald said, "All right, God damn it, you can come if General Clark says it is all right. Smith, take this man over to General Clark and see if he knows him and if he says he can come with us."

General Smith and I then got out of the plane and into Colonel Eddy's car, and drove across the airfield to a point where General Clark, General Grunther, and Elliot Roosevelt were standing. General Grunther darted forward, held out his hand, and said, "I am General Grunther." This friendliness pleased me. General Clark nodded to me wisely, and told General Smith very laconically that it was okay to take me. Elliot Roosevelt said nothing. General Smith and I went back to General Fitzgerald's plane, and we took off.

General Fitzgerald's attitude toward me at first, shall I say, was reserved; but as time went on he thawed and later apologized to me for his earlier unfriendliness. I did not blame him in the least; I had a hell of nerve. But I was ill and I wanted to get to Casablanca, particularly since Colonel Rattay wanted to see me and Browne about new developments in our Riffian guerrilla scheme and Browne was to await me there.

We stopped first at Tafaroui, and a galaxy of shoulder stars assembled under the wing of a four-motored bomber. There were Generals Clark, Doolittle, Grunther, Freydental, Fitzgerald, Smith, and Grant. General Doolittle greeted me in a friendly manner, since I had dined with him in Gibraltar.

At length we took our seats again, and took off; soon I was surprised to see that we were heading not west but south. Before long we were flying over desert, and I asked General Fitzgerald where we were gong. He answered, "Colomb Bechar."

This was all right with me; I would be glad to see Colomb Bechar, but I hoped we would not stay there long. We arrived before noon, and were greeted at the airfield by a French colonel, in charge of the post. He was a short, well-built man who walked very erect; he had on bright red riding boots and gloves, a sky-blue hat, and a blue uniform. He had bright golden hair, a bristly golden mustache, bright blue eyes, and a pair of thick-lensed pince nez glasses. He bowed from the waist and greeted the generals with elaborate courtesy. I had to do most of the interpreting.

He whipped the generals off to his house, and the rest of us were transported to the officers' mess. After lunch we returned to the plane, and General Fitzgerald announced that we were to fly directly, in a straight line, to Casablanca. I said that it would be better to go north a bit, follow the Moulouya valley upstream, and cross the pass over the Middle Atlas where the motor road from

Meknes to Midelt went; he said no, that they would just climb high in the air and swoop over the crests. Arthur Reed, another civilian passenger who was an oil vice-consul and who also had lived long in Morocco, sided with me, but we were swept aside.

The plane climbed and climbed and soon we were over clouds and dipping in and out of cloud banks. General Smith, who had been a high executive of American Airlines and was used to conservative passenger flying, began to sweat. My ears were very uncomfortable. Ice began to form on the wings, and the generals began to go in and out of the pilot's cabin. Soon we wheeled, and began a rapid descent. General Smith sweated even more profusely, and I felt a piercing pain in my left ear, which increased until I fell out of my seat, onto the floor, and lost consciousness.

When I recovered we were over desert again, and soon we landed once more at Colomb Bechar, in a torrent of rain. We proceeded back to the hotel, which was also the officers' mess, and were assigned quarters for the night. I was to sleep in a room in a private house, with Arthur Reed.

In the hotel there were many American Air Force officers, concerned with setting up the airport. There was also a high yellow girl from Brooklyn who called herself Mara Mara and who claimed to be a Hindu. To support this contention she exhibited a Kashmir frock that she claimed her grandmother had brought her from India. She had a French husband somewhere in the desert, and had been in Colomb Bechar two years. Needless to say, she was delighted with the presence of the flying officers, and more than delighted with the *deus-ex-machina* arrival of three generals simultaneously.

There seemed to be a shortage of bedding, and it was very cold, so the generals decided they wanted blankets. I led them on an expedition to the native market, and this procession of one American in a suit six sizes too big for him (I had lost fifty pounds), followed by three generals and a half-dozen colonels, drew a crowd. When we reached the suks, the procession halted. I found a blanket merchant with a large stock of native hand-woven woolen blankets, on sale for $14 each. Each of the passengers immediately wanted one, and General Fitzgerald wanted two. However, we could not buy them without bons, so a French officer who had appeared, dashed off, returning shortly with the appropriate official, who provided us with the necessary tickets, and the procession reformed, returning to the hotel with its blankets over its arms.

That night at dinner I was initiated to the short-snorter club, which cost me $18. Arthur Reed refused to join, whereupon General Fitzgerald told him that he would throw him off the plane; however, Arthur won, but the general's distaste for me was transferred to the stubborn vice-consul.

The next morning we took off again, and this time the pilot followed the route that Reed and I had indicated. It was not long before we were over Meknes, and at the general's orders we circled the airport, but we did not land. On the way I showed the general my billfold, made in Fez, and the general decided that he wanted to go there.

Later on we arrived at Rabat, and landed. After refueling, the general told me that he was going to Marrakech instead of to Casa, and that if I would stick with him he would arrive at Casa eventually. I was not sure that he would not first go to Fez, so Reed and I left, after many thanks for a pleasant voyage, and proceeded to town, where the army sent us to Casa on a jeep. Thus ended a very interesting journey.

After this I spent a week in bed in the Hotel Excelsior, with pneumonia.

On December 9 I visited Tangier for my next-to-the-last time, and stayed there three days. Colonel Eddy was there, and I went up to confer with him. He assigned me definitely to Algiers, where I joined the Massingham mess at Cap Matifou. There I stayed until Christmas.

Massingham is a British operation group concerned with the

penetration of Southern Europe. Its personnel came out shortly after the initial landing, and set up shop in a number of villas at Cap Matifou. For some time there was doubt whether it was to be purely British or Anglo-American; meanwhile I was assigned to it as Colonel Eddy's personal representative, as the only American. I ate and slept at the mess, but in the daytime served as instructor for the Corps Franc d'Afrique at Ain Taiya. The British took me in very warm-heartedly and I enjoyed my association with them very much. In fact, I liked them immensely and look back upon that period as a very pleasant one.

At the beginning I understudied Major Bruce and Captain Gubbins in their instructing at Ain Taiya. I had had little training in this and was very awkward. They were very tolerant and tried to help me. Soon it appeared that they were going to pull out and start instructing Massingham personnel at their new location at Club des Pins; I was to be left with the Corps Franc alone. Hence I chose six Frenchmen to serve as instructors, and proceeded to train them intensively, but we had trouble because of the lack of materials. I arranged for these to be delivered, and got permission to blow up a wrecked landing barge on the beach. Meanwhile the pupils were sent forward and we were awaiting a new lot.

At that time I wore British battle dress with a blue Corps Franc cap; when I went to Algiers I went in civilians. I drove my Studebaker with Consulat d'Amerique plates; all in all I occupied an extremely anomalous position and often had to go into lengthy explanations with British MPs to get past them to the Matifou mess.

My instructing at Ain Taiya was brought to an abrupt end on the day before Christmas. A former member of our camp at Ain Taiya assassinated Darlan; Captain Sabbatier, the head of the camp, hid for several days and then went to jail; my instructors either hid or were jailed, and the camp and my instruction program blew up.

Then Colonel Eddy sent me to Constantine to see Springs and

find out what was going on with the Anstruther's mission in Tunisia. On the way I got into trouble briefly. At Setif I stopped for gasoline, and went to see Colonel Saltzman, who was in charge. He was not available, but I was taken to see a Major Caesar Grazelli, his second-in-command. Major Grazelli asked for my passport, and seeing that it had expired six days before (it was then December 26 and the passport expired December 20), he told me that I should by rights be arrested and deported. We had a few words until Colonel Saltzman walked in; when he discovered that I was a Harvard professor and a friend of one of his professor friends, he calmed down Major Grazelli and gave me the gasoline.

I found Springs, saw Consul General Hooker Doolittle (my brother's father-in-law), and Springs and I decided that he (Springs) should return to Algiers with me. The trouble, as I discovered, was to a considerable extent due to Doolittle's personal antipathy to Springs and his (Doolittle's) failure to understand what we were up to, which was only natural since our activities were supposed to be secret in nature.

On January 1, Colonel Eddy and I drove to Guelma, with Springs and his chauffeur in another car. At Guelma we dined with Lieutenant Colonel Anstruthers, who agreed to send me to Tunisia as a member of his mission; the next morning I left for Jebel Halluf while Colonel Eddy and Springs returned to Algiers. Upon this as upon so many other occasions Colonel Eddy demonstrated that tact and ability to smooth over difficult situations, which is so important an element in his powers of leadership and organization. And thus ended the most hectic and least fruitful period in my year in North Africa.

C H A P T E R   F O U R

Special Detachment

Historical Setting: January and February 1943

THE sojourn at the outposts, especially Cap Serrat, appears to
have been an almost unqualified success, in spite of the danger
and the succession of demoralizing incidents. The OSS history
singles it out for particular mention in its general account of
North African operations. Cap Serrat is on the northwest coast of
the Tunisian peninsula. British, Free French, and American
forces, in that order, were to the south and west of it, but it was in
enemy territory, or perhaps no-man's land. The local French garrison adhered to the loyalty of its patriarch commander rather
than to the collaboration of Admiral Esteva.

Although Coon did not know it when he wrote, the two Arabs
he trained so carefully in railroad sabotage were spectacularly successful. They not only blew up a railway bridge, but did so while a
German troop train was on it. In this section one gets a specific
sense of the importance of what Coon has been talking about in
general terms, the differences as well as likenesses among the native peoples, and the need to know what they are. Here, too, is a
rare glimpse of the actual working of the system of gifts and hostages.

Coon does not discuss the German line of approach to the

Arabs with which he and his colleagues were in competition, although implicit in what he says is the recognition that there was
such a thing, distinct from French colonialism. The German ap-
peal was not based on anything as abstract as the Four Freedoms.
It was anti-Jewish, of course, but it also had a lot to do with the
revival of Islamic glory and Arab power in a German-run scheme
of things. The idea had great strength, as the postwar world has
seen.

Fighting in Tunisia

ON January 1, 1943, Colonel Eddy, Vice-Consul Springs, and I
went from Algiers to Maillot, where we spent the night, and the
next day proceeded to Guelma, where we dined in the hotel with
Colonel Anstruthers. Colonel Anstruthers agreed to accept me as
a member of the Special Detachment and instructed me to proceed to Djebel Hallouf the next day. (From now on Djebel Hallouf will be called Pig Hill, its literal translation, as commonly
used by members of the Detachment).

Early the next morning, Colonel Eddy, Springs, and I reported
at the Villa Baranger, Colonel Anstruthers' headquarters. I was
instructed to proceed in an automobile driven by a soldier of the
Special Detachment named Levy.* On the road to Pig Hill we
stopped for lunch at Souk Ahras, whence we crossed the range of

---

* Levy is a young Jew from Saarbruecken, and Levy is not his real name.
He claims to be a Count and to be the son of a wealthy owner of a chain
of jewelry stores throughout France. He also claims to have been a member of a Himalayan mountain climbing expedition. Levy will be considered in greater detail later, but I would point out at this juncture that he
was discovered to be one of the greatest swindlers in northern France,
and raped three Arab women, was condemned to death, and is now lan-
guishing in a medieval dungeon at Tabarka. It is my personal opinion
that this man should have been shot publicly in front of the Arabs whose
wives he had raped.

mountains between Algeria and Tunisia and came down through many curves to the flat plain that stretches from Ghardimaou eastward to the sea. From Ghardimaou to Souk el Arbaa is a veritable Messerschmidt alley. It is the habit of our Teutonic friends to spray this straight and narrow passageway with machine-gun bullets daily. My friend Levy stepped on the accelerator and whipped me to Souk el Arbaa as rapidly as possible. From Souk el Arbaa we continued on this death's highroad to Souk el Khemis, where we turned left over extremely bumpy road to Special Detachment Headquarters at Pig Hill.

Pig Hill is a lead-mining center, and several buildings of the lead-mining organization have been requisitioned by the Allied Forces. The largest has become a British hospital, one smaller building serves as SD offices, another is the store, while a third is used as an officers' mess. Upon my arrival at Pig Hill early in the afternoon I was turned over to Major Hamish Torrance, a small and wiry Scotsman with a huge curly mustache and a loud voice. Major Torrance had been in the Norwegian campaign and had made a number of parachute jumps in Norway and France. His nerves had been affected as a result of his experiences. Even then he was extremely jumpy, and later on this nervous state increased to such an extent that he had to be removed from Pig Hill for a rest. Major Torrance stated that I should visit the outposts of the Northern Section one by one, to acquaint myself with the way in which the Special Detachment was working. He advised me to go first to Post I.A., which is Cap Serrat, since this had been functioning longest and most effectively. I spent one night at Pig Hill before proceeding to this station.

Much to my surprise, Major Torrance addressed me as "colonel" and "sir" and showed me the utmost solicitude. That evening at the mess this was extremely embarrassing because Squadron Leader "Bombshell" Mallory was present and said: "Carl, congratulations! When were you promoted?" Major Torrance eyed me curiously but said nothing. Later I was able to take

Bombshell aside and told him that this colonelcy was as unknown to me as to him and I was at a loss to explain Major Torrance's use of this title. In order to get the matter straight I finally got Torrance aside and asked him why he was calling me colonel. He replied that he had been instructed that a retired American colonel named Coon was visiting the Detachment, and that as Colonel Anstruthers had said I was a colonel, it must be true. I said nothing, and thought that Colonel Anstruthers must have arranged for me to use this title as cover. I could not understand, however, why he had not told me about it in advance so that I could have played the part properly. This cover—if cover it was intended to be—was useless, since I kept encountering people like Bombshell, whom I had previously known in Gibraltar and who knew full well that I was not a colonel, so I soon discarded it.

At this point I should like to say a few words about the personnel of the Pig Hill post. Major Torrance was in command, and under him were two permanent appointments, Lieutenant Excell, and Lieutenant Ritchie. Excell is a big strapping Yorkshireman who was for a long time a sergeant of the British Police in Palestine. He speaks fluently both Hebrew and Palestinian Arabic. He is a security officer attached to Major Torrance, and has charge of interviewing Arab prisoners and hostages. As far as I can tell, he is doing an excellent piece of work. Ritchie, on the other hand, is a handsome young lad in his early twenties who is really an Arab and pretends to be French. He is a native of Tunis and has been to school in France and England. He was put into battle dress and given two green pips with the idea that he would be of use in infiltrating into Tunisia. However, the major has not so employed him as yet, and Ritchie serves in the capacity of adjutant. His ability to keep accounts and look after stores is only rudimentary and consequently he is always getting into trouble. Torrance's favorite evening exercise is to bawl Ritchie out in front of the other officers, to which Ritchie replies always: "Yes, Sir." "Yes, Sir." This is a form of sadism and masochism which both seem to enjoy. In my opinion, Ritchie has been completely misemployed.

Pig Hill was the center and headquarters of five Northern posts as follows:

I.A.   Cap Serrat, in charge of Lieutenant Richards
1.   Sedjanane, in charge of Lieutenant McAndrews
2.   Sidi Nsir, in charge of Captain Connors
3.   Oued Zarga, in charge of Captain Worrell
4.   El Aroussa, at that time in charge of Captain Lovatt

Captain Lovatt has subsequently been withdrawn to his own regiment and replaced by Lieutenant Adams. More will be said about these individual posts later; at this point it suffices only to mention that the only one of the posts' commanders who had had SOE training is Richards. The others were officers drawn from different regiments who were unaware of the existence or purpose of our organization, and consequently, however competent they may have been, they were incapable of appreciating our motives, and insisted on organizing our men in an infantry capacity. This failure to staff the posts with men from our organization had much to do with the character of the work performed in those places.

That afternoon I was given a car and a driver named Avril, a small, rotund Frenchman from the Massif Central, who conducted me to Sedjanane by way of Souk el Arbaa and Tabarka. He had never been over the road before and was in considerable perplexity, particularly during the latter part of the journey, when we were obliged to travel in the dark without lights. Between Djebel Abiod and Sedjanane we passed an unexploded bomb in the middle of the road, which had recently been dropped from an airplane. Several Royal Engineers were engaged in extracting it. Meanwhile traffic was greatly delayed and we were obliged to drive within a few inches of the bomb. When we eventually reached Sedjanane and found Lieutenant McAndrews' headquarters, I was shown into a small smoke-filled room in which a company of officers, some of them commandos, was crowded. Lieutenant Richards, whom I recognized despite his luxuriant beard, arose and explained to the others: "Here's Carl Coon; now the company of rogues and cutthroats is complete." They all arose at my entrance, tipping the table over and spilling all their food and drinks onto the tiled floor. After the confusion had ended, I was introduced to a number of people, including Colonel Glendinning, in charge of the commandos, and a tall Dracula-like figure with a bushy mustache named Lieutenant Colonel Trevor, who kept stroking his whiskers as he leaned over the fireplace with a glass in one hand. Another individual, who was very silent during the evening, was a redheaded Australian surgeon named Dr. Chin, who figures subsequently in this narrative.

The next morning Lieutenant Richards, Dr. Chin, and I went by truck to Sidi Meshrig by the motor road which leads to Cap Serrat. There we engaged in stripping a Stuka, which had recently fallen in a grove of fig trees. Two of the trees had been snapped off at the trunks and this annoyed the owner, the Sheikh, considerably. The Sheikh eventually produced a number of horses, and we proceeded on our way to Cap Serrat. This is a journey of four hours on foot. The horses were extremely scrawny and were covered with saddle sores.

At this point something should be said about the transportation situation between Cap Serrat and the outside world. Cap Serrat is thirty-five kilometers from Sedjanane to which post it is connected by a dirt road. At the time of our arrival at Cap Serrat, German patrols had successfully mined this road in several places, and upon the last attempt of light vehicles to go over it, a Bren-carrier had blown up, and the army was unwilling to allow vehicles to travel on that road with men or supplies. The only other road was the one to Sidi Meshrig, where we used the Hotel des Deux Plages as a junction post. This hotel belongs to the Lemaitre family of whom two members were in residence, Edmond and his fifteen-year-old brother, Charlot. Both of them were subsequently placed in SD uniform. Both personnel and supplies were brought to Sidi Meshrig by truck from Sedjanane.

At Sidi Meshrig the procedure was to ask the Sheikh, who was locally called "corporal," to supply horses. He did this by sending runners around the various gourbis to produce their horses and take us up. The horses that arrived were in such poor condition from overwork and starvation that usually we rejected two or three at sight out of every ten, and on the way we usually had to shift loads and send one or two back again. The total equine population of Sidi Meshrig has never been more than twenty, and of those at last sight only about six were in condition to carry men and material to Cap Serrat. Subsequently we obtained a certain amount of fodder for these horses from Major Haydon, and we also secured three mules shortly before the evacuation of the post. Those of us who made this journey usually preferred to walk part of the way since the horses were slow and extremely unsatisfactory. This technique of transportation made our supply systems extremely vulnerable. If the Italians had so wished, they could have cut the path which we took almost at will, and have isolated us completely from the outside world, particularly since sea approach was impossible during the months of January and February owing to the high winds and the condition of the water.

Returning to the narrative: Richards, Dr. Chin, and I started up the road to Cap Serrat on the available horses. Dr. Chin, however, refused to ride his, since it was in too poor condition, and walked, whereupon an Arab jumped on its back. This was invariably the procedure: as someone dismounted from a horse to spare it, someone else got on it. When we arrived at the next group of gourbis, one of our men ran across the countryside and shouted for another horse, and finally secured one, but Dr. Chin refused to ride this one also, much to the amazement of the Arabs, who proceeded to use this one as well for their own transport.

Before coming on this trip I had been told that one of the chief reasons for our difficulty in infiltrating people through the Italian lines was the telegraph system by which the natives shouted to one another from hilltop to hilltop and mountainside to mountainside, warning others in advance of our approach. Since none of the people who had reported this system had known Arabic, I was extremely skeptical from the start. On this first journey, one such shouting was noted, but I found out that it was merely a man who was looking for a horse for Dr. Chin, shouting all over the valley in an attempt to secure one, and could in no way be construed as a hostile warning. On all other occasions when I heard this shouting taking place some normal explanation could be found. In one instance a man was shouting to his son across the valley: "Hey, you young fool, bring in the goats for supper." In another case a boy was shouting to a she-goat to induce her to "ma'a" in reply, so that he could locate her. Shouting over long distances is the normal procedure for these Arabs and is an essential part of their daily activities. Whereas I do not state that our men have never been exposed by this method, I am sure that I have never witnessed this procedure, and I believe that in many cases in which it has been observed, the signals had nothing to do with us.

When we arrived at Ziatine, the village at the foot of Cap Serrat hill, we were met by one of our patrols who challenged us in the dusk. Upon recognition they let us through, and we proceeded up the hill to the lighthouse, where we retired. The post had been left in charge of Lieutenant John Adams Warren.

The personnel of Cap Serrat from this moment had consisted of Lieutenant Richards, a twenty-four-year-old scholar who had graduated from Cambridge with a first in English literature, and who had previously been concerned in sea operations of the English Channel. Lieutenant Richards speaks French perfectly, and has an outstanding ability in handling French personnel, so much so that the enlisted men on his staff were extremely loyal to him.

He showed outstanding ability and personal courage in his management of this very difficult post over a period of more than two months, and deserves great credit for his distinguished effort.

Under him was Lieutenant Warren, the son of an American father and British mother, born in England but brought up in California, who joined the Life Guards at the age of seventeen, served seven years in those ranks, then joined the Foreign Legion. At the outbreak of the present war he attempted to leave the legion and join the British Army. For this nefarious action he was condemned to a life internment at Maison Carrée at Algiers. After serving eighteen months in this gaol, the Allied troops entered Algiers and opened the doors of the prison. Warren proceeded to Constantine and Bône to join Richards, where he was made an officer in the Special Detachment. Warren concerned himself chiefly with personnel and their requirements. He was responsible for the routine; he carried out morning inspection, assigned groups for patrol, and in general took charge of the normal functioning of the camp, whereas Richards was more concerned with intelligence and preparing for special operations.

Dr. Chin fitted himself immediately into the group and opened a clinic for the care of our own personnel, and of the natives of the surrounding area. He lacked at first medical supplies for this, but obtained them later from Bône. He was subsequently able, on this account, to save the life of Lieutenant Warren and of a number of RAF personnel who featured in subsequent action. He was also able to administer to the needs of many Arabs, and this had an outstanding effect upon our relations with the native population. Dr. Chin's action, as much as anything else, helped to change our relations with the Arabs from unfriendly to friendly, and it is earnestly recommended that more medical clinics of this type be set up all around the front wherever possible.

My own duties were more elastic. I had charge of interviewing hostages and prisoners, also of giving out supplies of cloth, tea, sugar, and so forth, and of whatever demolition activities were necessary, aside from the special jobs done by the Captains Eyre and Gubbins. It was my nightly duty to set booby traps in the area on either side of the bridge that was our last outpost against the Italians. On one occasion, during the illness of Lieutenant Warren and in the absence of Lieutenant Richards, I was in actual command of the post for a few days.

The normal routine at Cap Serrat included maintaining a lookout at all times upon the semaphore, maintaining a guard through the night at the bridge, and sending out patrols into the wide expanse of no-man's land stretching between us and the Italians. The country consists of three types of environment; wide sand dunes stretching far inland, forests of scrub oak reaching to the shoulder and affording abundant cover for anyone willing to keep his head down; and cork forests in which one can walk unobserved at a certain distance, though visibility between the trunks was greater than that in the scrub country. This country is ideal for patrol operations, for a small party can move within a few yards of the enemy unobserved and can remain in hiding during the day with little chance of observation. This advantage of course was enjoyed by both sides. The Italians could creep up within a few yards of our position at the bridge without the slightest difficulty. Similarly our patrols could duck under the bushes and hide successfully when a large Italian patrol approached.

During my stay at Cap Serrat, our operation took three forms: *Defensive, Observational,* and *Offensive.*

Defensive operations included manning the semaphore, manning the bridge and, later on when the river dried, manning the beach, as well as my special activities in setting booby traps, signal wires, rockets and so on, so that we could be warned of the enemy's approach.

Observational activities consisted in looking over the country at the semaphore with powerful glasses, in sending out patrols for information, and in the use of Arab watchers and informers who kept us fairly well advised of the movements of the enemy. We had two watchers on the hill between the bridge and Chirane at all times, prepared to warn us by the use of incendiaries by day, and either lighthouse sky rockcts or Verey lights at night. Similarly we rigged a green sky rocket in the window of Commandant Perrin's house so that if his family were attacked by the enemy he could let us know immediately. Up to the time of my departure the commandant had not needed to use this signal. As for the enemy, we soon learned that they had two main camps, one at Mhabbes on the Kef Abbed Peninsula, and the other at the ford over the Oued Harka. Each of these consisted of 250 to 300 men. There were two other posts between Oued Harka and Sedjanane.

Offensive operations were few in number and small in scope due to the small size of our garrison. We could not afford to risk the loss of personnel. Our total strength averaged from thirty to fifty men of whom many were often on the sick list because of overfatigue and malnutrition, as well as the fact that they all had been previously in jail and had had no time to recover their health before entering our service. They were constantly pricking their hands, feet, and legs on the huge thorns so abundant in that area, and suffering from infection. Others suffered from scabies, and one man was a mess of sores from this parasite. Others had fevers and abdominal cramps and other ailments, and it was often necessary to send them back to Pig Hill as unfit for service. One man sent up from Pig Hill was cross-eyed; he had lost his glasses several months earlier and was unable to see, and we had to send him back again. Why he was sent to us in the first place in this condition I cannot understand. One group of four men sent to us as Spaniards turned out to be Italians, and one of these had wounded legs so that he could not walk more than 100 yards. He too had to be returned along with the other Italians, none of whom were trusted to operate against their fellow countrymen. For these various reasons, offensive operations were limited to several mining expeditions in enemy territory, and they will be described later.

Discipline was fairly good, in view of the circumstances, although individuals often took it upon themselves to act without orders. One man, Eustache, who was a group leader, pilfered the semaphore flags from the tower and used them for himself and his men as neckerchiefs, handkerchiefs, gun wipers, and toilet paper. The cook, in fact, used the yellow quarantine flag for a hand towel. On one occasion Eustache and his group slept at their post by the bridge, and Lieutenant Richards, coming down at 6 a.m., took their Bren gun away from them amid loud snores. He hid it in the bushes and they had to ask him where it was when they awoke. For these various defections from duty, Eustache was relieved of his command and sent back to Pig Hill.

Another man, Matenet, was on guard on the bridge on one occasion when an Arab came over it with the announcement that 500 or 600 Italians had passed through Chirane and were approaching. Matenet, who was no Horatius, handed his Bren to the Arab and fled, leaving the bridge unguarded. The Arab then met Dr. Chin and myself, who were on our way down to set booby traps, with the same announcement. We proceeded to the bridge where I set our booby traps, while Chin guarded me with Sten and hand grenades. The mythical army turned out to be our own commandos returning from a foray, as Chin and I had expected. Matenet was sent back to Guelma, where he was tried and last seen doing a camp fatigue duty. Matenet is probably insane and should either be exterminated or placed in a mental hospital.

Considering the conditions under which these men live, the constant strain and the lack of relief, as well as the fact that this group, varying in numbers from seventeen to fifty, was holding the whole northern pivot of the Allied line against ten or twenty times their number of Italians, it is no wonder that events such as I have described occurred occasionally. This is particularly true when one considers that few of these men had had any previous military training. Many of them were excellent people from every point of view. Durand, one of the group leaders, Marshal, and

Cross, were outstanding in courage, leadership, and technical ability.

Upon my arrival there was only one French officer present, Lieutenant Mahouzies. Lieutenant Rageneau, who had broken his glasses, had had to be sent to Constantine for a new pair, and did not return for two weeks. Mahouzies is a very eccentric individual. He was once a Trappist Monk and was also at one time in the printing business. He is physically unfortunate in possessing narrow shoulders, wide hips, and knock-knees, and the soldiers laughed at him behind his back for his peculiar gait. He lacks judgment completely and was constantly getting us into difficulty. At the end of my sojourn at Cap Serrat, Lieutenant Richards dismissed Mahouzies and sent him to Guelma, where he was returned as a private soldier to the Corps Franc d'Afrique. Rageneau, on the other hand, was an excellent soldier and held the respect of the men under his command.

There is one more Cap Serrat personality who deserves particular mention: the Commandant Perrin. Perrin is a seventy-year-old retired French Army officer, related to the family of Gants Perrin, famous in Paris. He came to Tunisia many years ago and bought the lowland around the mouth of the Ziatine River, making himself proprietor of the Ziatine village area, so that the inhabitants of that village became his retainers. He is a rare Frenchman of the highest type, a man of supreme courage, great learning, and noble character. He regards the natives under him as his direct responsibility and treats them with rare benevolence and understanding. His presence in the Cap Serrat area is of utmost importance to our local war effort. Lieutenant Richards wisely recognized his value and spent two to three hours each day consulting with the commandant. Beside the commandant, there is Mme. Perrin, Perrin's son Jacques, and Perrin's twenty-two-year-old daughter. All except Jacques are in bad health, the two women suffering acutely from malaria. Jacques' wife and children were evacuated by horse on the day we arrived; we passed them on the road, riding along with the family of the lighthouse keeper, who also departed that day.

Dr. Chin, realizing the importance of medical and surgical work in that area, left after a couple of days for Tabarka and Bône to get together the necessary supplies. Richards and I stayed there one week. During this time the routine of the post proceeded normally. Aside from this, we were subjected to constant alerts and on one occasion were badly machine-gunned by a Messerschmidt. Luckily no one was injured. My duties consisted of building up the defense of the bridge over the Ziatine by booby traps, installing a signal system for the farm, and interviewing Arabs. My booby-trap program, although it took much time, was not a great success. I caught no Italians that I know of, the total casualties being one Arab and one cow. One day I set many traps in the woodpile cutoff to the right of the road beyond the bridge, a favorite place for the enemy to sneak up. I finished just at dusk, having also set three-alarm signals on and before the bridge. Having just finished and retired to our side of the bridge, I heard one trap go off, and we all ducked into the bushes. Then another, and then an Arab, one of our signalmen, dashed through the gap, his legs going like pistons, his hands clutched to the back of his head. Before we could stop him he came through all three signal wires, producing a pop, pop-pop, pop-pop-pop! and collapsed at our feet. He had only one small Mills-bomb fragment in the back of his head, though he had put off three grenades. Dr. Chin patched him up and he insisted on going home to let his wife know that he was alive. Later he returned for treatment and was soon fully healed.

When I arrived, we had a number of prisoners in the care of a sadist named Simeon, who was rightly named; facially he resembled a chimpanzee. He had been knocked around in the Foreign Legion and was now taking it out on helpless Arabs. These were made to sleep in a stinking watercloset without enough room to lie down and without sufficient bedding. He led them out on fatigue duty each day, to clean the privies, to clean out our mess, to chop wood with a mattock, and he periodically smacked them with a piece of rubber hose, which I soon took away from him. I saw to it that the prisoners were placed in more humane quarters, and turned over to Halimi, a Jew of Constantine, rather than to Simeon. Halimi was much more humane and understanding, and became my number-one assistant in Affaires Indigenes.

Our program of sweetening the Arabs was greatly hampered by our use of French personnel. They distrust Arabs and vice versa, and could not understand our attitude. They were constantly and most annoyingly advising us not to trust Arabs, and they at times took away presents we had given the Arabs as being too good for them. The worst of all were Levy and two associates, who on three occasions entered Arab gourbis while on patrol, disrobed the Arabs of both sexes, and took turns raping the naked Arab women while the other two men held the rest of the people at bay with sten guns. They were sent back to Guelma via Pig Hill; Torrance told the Pig Hill garrison that they had been shot. This could not be done because of our arrangements with the French. Torrance, however, arranged with Quiliquini to have them thrown in the old Tabarka dungeon for the duration. Then Colonel Anstruthers by mistake sent them back to Pig Hill, much to Torrance's ire and chagrin.

One man whom they were mistreating was an Arab picked up near the Lusanchi farm by Group Leader Gross. Gross saw the man sitting alongside the road holding an antiquated shotgun. Gross began talking German, whereupon the Arab stated that the Germans were good and the British and French bad. Gross led him to the lighthouse where he had been beaten daily until my arrival, and was to be shot. I interviewed the man, gave him cigarettes and tea, and calmed him down. He stated that he was a small farmer of the Sedjanane region, that he was out looking for his stray goats when taken, and that he carried the fowling piece (without ammunition) because he was a professional guide for European bear hunters and always carried it. He had praised the

Germans because he thought Gross was a German (Gross is from Lorraine) and he wanted to live. If he had deemed Gross British, he would have praised the British, etcetera. After all, it was the country of the Moslems and he wanted only to live in peace. I let him go, with presents, on parole to the Sedjanane bureau. This man had been irretrievably injured through French malice and general stupidity and there was little that could be done in the way of amends.

Then there were the three brothers Ben Khemis from Cap Negro: Hasona, Yussuf, and Mabruk. All three were bachelors working to support their aged parents. Mahouzies had taken them prisoner at Cap Negro and brought them to Cap Serrat. The charge was that they had a great quantity of mixed cartridges, mostly British, in their gourbi. They also had some cans of gasoline. When I questioned them separately, without giving them the chance to communicate with each other until it was all over, they told between them a consistent story, with enough differences to account for individual differences of observation and to prevent the possibility of a rehearsed tale.

Hasona was a mason's helper in Bizerta. Yussuf was the doorkeeper of the brothel of Mme. Andre Cinzano in Bizerta. Mabruk was a woodcutter at home. Every so often, usually about once a month, Mabruk went to Bizerta to collect money from his two brothers for their parents. On his way home from such a journey he passed the battlefield of Djebel Abiod and found some cartridges, which he loaded on his donkey and took home. He opened a few to see if the powder could be used in his father's ancient fowling piece, but seeing an unfamiliar type of explosive decided that it could not. He intended to turn the cartridges over to the Controlleur Civil during his next official visit. The gasoline had washed up on the shore, and all the villagers had gone out to retrieve it. The Controlleur Civil had told them on his last visit that flotsam and jetsam should be collected, one half held for the government, one half kept. They had divided the gasoline into two parts, one cached on the beach for the government, the other half distributed in the houses. Mabruk intended to do the same with the ammunition.

As a solution to this case, we kept Yussuf as messboy, Hasona as cook's assistant, and sent Mabruk home, to come back periodically to collect his brothers' wages and give us information. The two with us were to receive the same pay as in Bizerta. This arrangement was eminently satisfactory; the two with us worked well, Mabruk brought excellent information, as well as hens, and eggs. Unfortunately Hasona was killed in a machine-gunning after I had left, and I do not know where Yussuf went when our force evacuated the post. I had planned to use him in Bizerta for intelligence if his job could be got back. We were waiting to hear from our W/T man in Bizerta.

Space forbids details of all our hostages, but we found that when we entered a distant village where loyalty was wavering, we could take the eldest son of the most important man and hold him in the lighthouse pending his father's arrival. The old man inevitably came, with gifts, demanding his son. He was sent back to get good information of enemy positions, and when he came the second time his son would be released if the information were satisfactory. With one exception, this system worked, and the sons in most cases became acclimatized to the garrison life and liked it there. This use of hostages was our chief source of intelligence aside from the work of our own patrols.

Our most useful man of all was Brahim, an ex-Tirailleur who had escaped from prison in Germany. He went at once (after my arrival) to Mateur, Ferryville, and elsewhere, selling eggs, and upon his return gave an accurate account of Italian positions, supply dumps, etcetera. Later I sent him and his friend Ali to blow the Tindja-Ferryville Railroad, and if possible to wreck the train. Lieutenant Robertson and I made up the charges at Mahouna, and Dr. Rossmiller sewed them in a packsaddle. The idea of using a packsaddle was originally that of Richards and Chin, who intended to use it for printed propaganda. I do not yet know whether or not Brahim wrecked his train. We trained him well at the Guelma Railroad, his load was well concealed, and he was an expert at infiltration. His whole scheme was carefully planned and if anything went wrong it was not from lack of planning and foresight.

Returning to Cap Serrat: Chin left after two or three days to get his supplies, Richards and I after a week. We went to Sedjanane via Sidi Meshrig and at Sedjanane mounted a truck with five prisoners, a British driver, and a British sergeant for Pig Hill. At the town of Djebel Abiod, just before the bridge, we saw five enemy aircraft approaching. We jumped, the prisoners scattered, two making for the hill to the left, the other three under the truck with Richards and others. I tried to run clear of the road, tripped, fell on my face in the mud, and was shot at; bullets landed very close to me. Then I got up and we ran into a building. A Stuka dive-bombed, aiming for the bridge which it barely missed. It made a crater 50 feet wide and 30 feet deep in the bank, the edge some 70 feet from us. The building tottered but held; a tile fell from the roof, hitting me on the head, and bouncing on to Lieutenant Richards' hand. I had on my gray felt hat, and soon an egg-sized lump arose on my pate.

Two of the prisoners had disappeared, and after a prolonged search we failed to recover them. From Pig Hill we went to Tabarka, where we picked up Dr. Chin and his bulky and valuable supplies, including a great deal of plasma. Before that we had reported to Corps at Suk el Khemis in an attempt to persuade them to give us regular troops. We were doing infantry work and had no time for our proper tasks.

At Tabarka we saw Quiliquini, the Controleur Civil, about opening markets to compete with Mateur and about one M. Armand of Sidi Meshrig. The market business eventually was handed over to Colonel Allen and Major Haydon, who have handled it very well. M. Armand is a besotted French colon near

Sidi Meshrig with an Australian wife in Tunis. Armand has long been at odds with the natives, and once when his farm was robbed seized eight cows from an innocent native. That native was dependent on the milk for his sustenance, and that of his family, and consequently was starving. Unfortunately our brave Lieutenant Mahouzies had helped Armand in this piece of injustice. Quiliquini promised to remove Armand from the area under arrest, but never did. I finally arrested him myself and sent him to Tabarka under armed guard.

When we got back to Sidi Meshrig, we found some deserters from the commandos skulking in the hotel and eating our supplies. Three American privates and one British sergeant, completely demoralized; they had started out for Cap Serrat with the others and got lost and returned. They refused to go on with us through fear that the post had been captured. They trumped up imaginary illnesses which Dr. Chin soon exposed. At Cap Serrat we found 100 Anglo-American commandos under Captain Craven, Lieutenant Davidson, and an American second lieutenant named MacFarlane, who had recently been promoted from sergeant. He wanted me to try the deserters as a consular officer, but never turned them over. He seemed to me very ineffectual.

That night the commandos decided to take over the guard at the bridge. For some reason which I cannot remember, other than that I was very tired, I failed to go down at dusk to set booby traps as usual. Lieutenant Warren and Captain Craven set out with six American commandos to take up the post. Now the system was up until that time that the bridge was observed by day from the semaphore; about 5:30 p.m. the guard went down for the night to man the Bren and hold the position. I usually went down before the guard to start my work. Dr. Chin usually went down with me to guard me, or failing him, one of the men.

That afternoon 200 Italians went to Chirane village, over the ridge, tied up all the natives, sneaked over the bridge about 3:30 p.m. and lay in ambush, either for me or the guard or both. When the guard came they threw percussion grenades, killing Privates Fifield and Parsons, capturing two other privates and Captain Craven, and leaving Lieutenant Warren for dead. The other two privates dived in the bush and stayed there. Lieutenant Richards, who was at the farm, heard the noise and dashed down. He found the two privates, left them, came back and got us who were awaiting supper. We went down (Richards, Davidson, Chin, myself, and commandos) and searched but found no trace of the four missing men, including Warren. Next morning Warren walked into the farm and collapsed. He had an Italian field dressing on his head, with the safety pin through his scalp. An Arab had picked him up and kept him in his gourbi all night. His pockets had been emptied, presumably by the Italians. Later we heard from natives that Craven and the two privates had been well treated once the captors found they were not French.

We buried Privates Fifield and Parsons near the bridge and set up a twenty-four-hour guard at the bridge.

The afternoon after the attack, Colonel Trevor and Captain Gubbins appeared. They had not heard of the attack. Gubbins and I went below to set traps. We set a good many, and started for the farm to plan the mining of the beach. On the way one of our traps went off, and we returned to the bridge to find the commandos (British this time) huddled in a tight group near the bridge in full view of the other side. We explained to them that they were very vulnerable, and *advised* (I being a civilian and Michael Gubbins not being a commando officer) them to spread out, and command the bridge from either side. Then we went back to warn Perrin, and returned toward the bridge. Near the scene of the previous night's attack we found the commandos together again under a fence, out of sight of the bridge, which was undefended. One man with a Bren was to the right of the road, the others to the left. We joined those on the left, heard voices ahead, saw moving objects, and deciding that little could be done with the existing force, we (Gubbins and I) went back to the lighthouse as quickly as possible and told Richards and Trevor. Trevor reprimanded Gubbins and myself, particularly me, for "giving an order" dispersing the men from the bridge; he blamed us, especially me, for their present position. He ordered out the whole commando, ordered Gubbins and me to proceed over 100 yards in advance of the commando to the Italian "position," or the place just to the left of the bridge where noises had been heard, and throw in magnesium flares. We lashed tysules to flares, took strikers, and started off. When we got within fifteen yards of the bridge we lit our flares, tossed them, and ducked. We found no trace of the Italians, but the booby that went off had apparently been set off by some instrument, for nearby we found a piece of metal which did not come from our equipment. They had presumably seen Gubbins and me setting the traps. Whether or not they had actually crossed the bridge as we had supposed we could not determine.

Returning to the lighthouse, we found Colonel Trevor comfortably slumbering in Lieutenant Richards' bed. He never went to the bridge at all, and next morning left early by the coast road, in Arab dress, on Richards' horse, with an Arab guide.

A few days later the commandos left, but not until after having carried out one patrol into no-man's land. This was to allow Gubbins to mine a marabout (a saint's tomb).

This brings me back to mining operations in general. Before this, the week before, Captain John Eyre had been sent up to mine the Lusanchi farm, where Arab patrols often spent the night. After elaborate planning between Richards and Perrin, it was decided that Captain Eyre was to use a piece of pig as trigger, to avoid killing Arabs. He set out with a patrol under Gross, with Ali ben Amor as guide, reached the farms, killed a pig, and rigged his trap. On the way back they were ambushed, and Ali ben Amor dropped a roll of Cordtex. Gross was nearly captured, shots were exchanged. The Italians were standing in the bushes with brush in their helmets and veils over their faces. Our men subsequently adopted these techniques. They arrived exhausted and intact. Later we heard that the Italians sent a man in to hitch a string to the meat, and detonated it from a distance, demolishing the building without loss.

The Gubbins operation was equally if not more unfortunate. He went out with the commandos to mine a marabout where the Italians convened. Richards was sure that the Arabs used it only in the fall. I was not so sure, since marabouts are curative and disease is not seasonal, but the superior local knowledge of Commandant Perrin seemed insuperable and I did not demur as loudly as I should have. Gubbins mined his marabout as directed. Later on an Arab woman and her son went there. The son dug a Hawkins out of the ground and played with it; the whole marabout went up, killing the boy and maiming the woman who, among other things, was blinded. A later patrol of ours brought in the father and older son as hostages; the son was held and the old man sent back to get information. He hesitated but went. He brought back secondhand but valuable information, was sent out again for more personal observations, and never returned. The Italians caught him. If he did not tell them all he could about us, I will be surprised, because we had not exactly treated him with the utmost consideration.

After another ten days or so I was summoned to Guelma by Colonel Anstruthers. After some opposition locally I left, for with the departure of the commandos I was needed. Gubbins was also supposed to leave, but he stayed on so that there would be someone conversant with boobies and demolition during my absence. Arriving at Pig Hill I met with a statement from Colonel Anstruthers that owing to the imminent arrival of General Gubbins (Captain Gubbins' father) I should stay at my post, so I returned to Cap Serrat. Meanwhile Major Torrance made me a captain

with three green pips; I took over the hat of the late Captain Ri-
tinitis who had blown himself up opening a box with a shell as
screwdriver, and hammering the cap; and thus accoutred I went
back by way of Sedjanane. I took with me Major Haydon, the
man who under Brian Clark gives out supplies, and Captain
Lovelock, of the Psychological Warfare.

When I got there, Richards was ordered back to corps to see
about getting more garrison, and I was left in command. One
night we had an alarm; our two watchers of the Ghiran ridge
begged off duty for fishy excuses. Ali ben Amor, whom the commandos wanted as a guide to meet them at Sidi Nasir el Aoud,
was loath to go; Arabs told Commandant Perrin that the Italians
were to attack that night. I found that the men on the semaphore
could see and hear nothing, so I posted a guard around the top of
the hill, and gave flares to the guard on the beach, since the water
in the river was low and natives were fording constantly at beach
level. Also the beach could not be seen directly through the bulge
of the hill overlooking the Perrin farm. There was much grum-
bling about this but I insisted. I had meanwhile been ordered
back to Guelma by Colonel Anstruthers but delayed twenty-four
hours for this purpose. Then the wireless went off and we ran out
of food; we had to send for goats to slaughter. In the morning, I
went to Sidi Meshrig, thinking to meet Richards with the provisions, as expected. When he did not appear I got on a mule which
had been sent there for him from Sedjanane, and trotted bareback
17 km. to the Sedjanane road, hopped a Bren carrier, and had
MacAndrews send the provisions right away by truck. The next
morning I went to Pig Hill where I found Richards still in process
of discussing reinforcements.

Colonel Young and Major Michael (Bing) Crosby arrived;
Richards went back; Young, Crosby, and I made a tour of the
Wed Zarga post, and I went back to Guelma with Colonel
Young, leaving Major Crosby in charge, understudying Torrance,

who was soon to go to the hospital whence he was eventually rusticated to Mahona.

One of our many visitors to Cap Serrat (it became a sort of tourists' Mecca) was Squadron Leader Brown, who wanted to set up a secret weapon there. He soon sent two RAF wireless men, and we also got a British coding clerk and a medical orderly for Dr. Chin. The coding clerk and medical orderly dug a latrine for the French, whose habit it was to defecate on the spot like apes; in one case they defecated at the top of the semaphore and pushed it over the edge with their feet. After I left Browne had the Sedjanane road decontaminated, and brought up an RAF company as garrison for his death ray.

Arriving at Guelma I was soon sent back with Colonel Young on a tour of the posts; with Major Crosby we visited el Aroussa, Sidi Nasir, and Sedjanane; then we got a Bren carrier and went up to Cap Serrat in it over the very badly chewed-up motor road, where we passed many stranded vehicles. We also passed Lieutenant Richards riding in a jeep in the company of the commodore and other naval officers on the way to Sedjanane whither he (Richards) had been summoned by the brigadier. The commodore had come to see about sea operations.

When we got to the neighborhood of the farm, we saw the RAF encamped. We went up to the lighthouse where we found Warren and Chin. We stayed for lunch, during which time Colonel Young decided that the position was untenable for us, particularly since the Italians would let no Arabs through because we had oversweetened them. And also because the enemy would certainly wreck the place once they found the RAF installed. It was no good for infiltration, and we had relief for our infantry duties. At long last we need no longer hold the northern pivot of the United Nations line.

We took Johnny Warren off in the Bren carrier, and proceeded to Sedjanane. Johnny and I and Crosby walked down the street,

Johnny with his beard and bandage looking like the *Spirit of '76.*
We got in a medico and he sent Johnny off to the hospital in
Bône, whence he was subsequently moved to Mahona.

Colonel Young and I went to Pig Hill and Guelma. On about
the 18th of February our men finally pulled out of Cap Serrat and
went to Mahona for a much needed rest, all but Dr. Chin who
stayed (and is to my knowledge still there) awaiting the arrival of
an RAF surgeon. The need for this was due to the attack the
enemy made by air on Cap Serrat a few days before the evacuation of our men. They machine-gunned the lighthouse, the farm,
the RAF camp, the village of Ziatine, and the Ziatine-Sidi-
Meshrig road. They killed Hasona, three RAF soldiers, several
Arabs of Ziatine, and one Arab woman on the trail. They
wounded a number of RAF personnel. They dropped a bomb
within a few feet of the lighthouse. Dr. Chin had to stay to care
for his wounded while others buried the dead. When he gets out
he deserves a long rest and a decoration.

Period two of my history is a stay of a few days at Guelma and
Mahona, where I ate and drank off the fat of the land, trained
Brahim and Ali to blow their train, trained another Ali sent by
Captain Worrell to lay antipersonnel mines, and prepared for the
southern campaign. It seems that Ali number two had been sent
by Worrell with an oral message, and I was to train him to take
out a German minefield of teller mines. I knew not how, nor did
any of the R. R.'s present. The idea was that Ali was to clear a
path in a field flanking a gun on a hill so that vehicles could make
a surprise attack. That seemed to me hardly SOE or OSS business, and to be due to Worrell's misconception of our functions.
So I trained him in antipersonnel, to get the animal supply trains
victualing this spot, and took him back to Pig Hill on my way to
the south, to clear the matter up in passing.

Dr. Rossmiller and Ali and I proceeded in my Studebaker to
Pig Hill. On the way we bucked two feet of snow in the passes,

and left 100 vehicles stranded. Only by the superior driving skill of the Doc were we able to leave the others behind us. The next day Colonel Young, who was present, had a meeting of all the post commanders, including MacAndrews, Connors, Worrell, and Adams (who replaced Lovatt), which was to become a weekly affair and a very excellent one indeed, since previously the commanders in many cases had not met. Worrell explained that what he had really wanted Ali number two to do was to learn how to lay Hawkins, which Worrell himself or anyone at Pig Hill could have taught him.

Historical Setting: Kasserine

THE major military engagement Coon takes part in, but never mentions by name, was the battle of Kasserine Pass. It was the first big fight between American and German troops and was a sharp, serious, but ultimately instructive defeat for the Americans. Officially, the battle lasted from February 18 to 23, but General Juergin von Arnim, the German commander in Tunisia, had been attacking in increasing strength for some time before that.

Late in 1942, when Eisenhower realized that he could not take Tunis in the winter weather with the forces at hand, he took up a position in Tunisia along a line running north and south, and for much of the distance along the slopes of a mountain range known as the Eastern Dorsal. In the north was the British First Army under General Kenneth Anderson. Then came a patchwork of Free French divisions and finally the American II Corps under General Lloyd Fredendall. The whole front was weak and II Corps was without its reserve units, which had been parceled out to strengthen other commands.

On February 18, von Arnim broke through the French at Faid Pass and continued on west, chewing up units of II Corps, pene-

trating Kasserine Pass, and heading for the supply center at Tebessa. He was held just west of Kasserine by American artillery
rushed 750 miles over icy mountain roads from Oran and British
tanks sent down from the north. (It was this British armor that
Coon struggled through on his way back to Algiers.) At this time,
General Montgomery and his Eighth Army launched a well-con-
ceived diversionary attack just east of Rommel's position in the
Mareth Line. In response to it, von Arnim withdrew his Panzers
from Kasserine on the 23rd and headed east to support Rommel.

For the Americans, the defeat uncovered deficiencies from as
high as corps command down to the handling of small units. The
principal failure seemed to be that in allowing his reserve forces to
be shifted to other commands, Fredendall had lost the power to
counterattack. Whether or not this was strictly his fault, it cost
him the confidence of his division commanders, and consequently
his job. Eisenhower replaced him with Patton.

For Coon and his companions, Kasserine must have been as
frustrating as it was for everyone else. When they had their comic
opera interview with Colonel Akers, everything was beginning to
fly apart in all directions. When they left for Algiers, there were
signs of recovery. In between, they obviously found something
more useful to do than to act as suicide infantry squads, but they
cannot have felt that they were well employed.

The most notable man in their company, for whom Coon did
not need to write a character assessment, was Major General
Colin Gubbins, the chief of SOE, who had been Donovan's men-
tor and was now his opposite number. Just before the outbreak of
war, Gubbins had been in Poland on the trail of the famous German Enigma cipher machine, and he had a hand in setting up the
formidable organization in the United States run by the Canadian
William Stephenson under the code name Intrepid. Later on,
Gubbins was superseded in his job during the shift in Allied policy toward the Balkans when Mihailovich was abandoned in favor
of Tito. On the Tunisian occasion, Gubbins should certainly not

have been wandering around loose in the middle of a fluid battle, but perhaps the encounter with Colonel Akers was worth it. Donovan was habitually even more foolhardy.

Special Detachment, continued

THENCE I proceeded via le Kef to the south, and at Tebessa, II Corps headquarters picked up Sergeant Byzek; I took Major Sage's Renault and he took my Studebaker, the reason being that I was following a lorry and could be retrieved if the Renault cracked, while the Studebaker being a good car could be counted on to stand the gaff alone. Quiney, Sage, Robertson, Robert, the four sergeants, and thirty-odd Spaniards had arrived the previous afternoon and were encamped at Cactus Castle above Sbeitia. We went to Cactus Castle. Later Byzek arrived; during his ride the Studebaker had developed an ominous knock.

Now it seems that the southern show had been lined up as follows: Captain Brandy-Rimmer had gone to Kasserine and gotten some thirty-odd members of the Loyalist Spanish Navy out of internment. More than 200 remained. He took them to Mahona. Then he cracked a car (a usual Guelma procedure) and went to the hospital for one month. Exit Brandy-Rimmer. Major Quiney (whom I have long known as master of the Villa Lourdes mess in Gibraltar), a twenty-eight-year-old major, was given charge of the training and use of these men.

Quiney's personality, in view of subsequent events, needs some elaboration. He is a mixture of Dunsany and Cervantes. He was born in Teneriffe, of an Irish family owning hotels, reared there and in England, and from his physical appearance must inevitably have Spanish blood. He is bilingual, bicultural, and individual. He has at all times a faraway look in his eyes. He is reserved and shy, but once you break the ice his intimacy is simple and charming. He is like an Aztec sacrifice to Huitzilopochtli, the god of war; he lives in ecstasy in anticipation of a glorious end. He is one of the bravest men I have ever known, and one of the most irresponsible. As a glorious individual and friend, I salute George Quiney, but as a leader of men I deplore him.

Several other personalities merit description before this narrative continues. Jerry Sage, Sergeant Byzek, Sergeants Goff, Milt Felsen, and Sergeant Lassowski, Captain Robert, Lieutenant Robertson, Lieutenant Crosby, Lieutenant Colonel Anstruthers, Lieutenant Colonel Young. If this be considered too personal, this part of the narrative may be omitted. But I consider it essential to the understanding of the events which followed. It is extremely objective, and in all cases, as in the case of Major Quiney, I feel personal affection for the individual involved.

Jerry Sage: Sage is a young man of extreme physical good fortune, tall, handsome, athletic, full of energy and of personal courage. He has all the traditional American virtues: loyalty and compassion and a keen sense of justice. He must have been a campus hero when he was in college. He is a fine parachutist, a great man with his hands, quick, agile, and fearless. He has a facile sense of humor but little depth of intelligence. He will spare his men but spend himself. And he irks at superior authority, always wants to take charge. Yet he is a soldier and will obey orders if they appear suicidal, once he is convinced of the regularity of the procedure. As a planner, he seems better than Quiney but leaves much to be desired. A Homeric hero, half berserk. With Quiney and Sage, we are in the midst of the *Iliad.* Added to this, we must remember that Sage, like Quiney, is fresh from the schools of war; he is anxious to practice the trade which he has so well learned, and so long awaited. He cannot await the clever, the discreet opportunity to smite the enemy with maximum effect; he must cut with sword and chariot at the first dust of battle; he is no Odysseus, he is an Achilles.

Sergeant Byzek: The big Bohunk, the Slovak from Hawaii. A huge handsome Slavonic American, the perfect Holy Cross

Fighting Irish. A young man of gigantic physique and boundless energy, full of wile; he rides a motorcycle perfectly; he can keep the convoy together, and can scout the countryside far and wide for tires, spare parts, woolen underwear, and medical supplies; the supreme scavenger and moocher, and bureau of information, completely reckless and completely practical. Wholly independent yet obedient to orders, the sergeant supreme. A jack of all trades, an improviser, always with a smile, never dismayed, fanatically loyal to Sage. A man to toss anywhere and land on his feet. A perfect American.

Sergeant Goff: A small, wiry idealist. A former tap dancer and vaudeville trouper, who fought in the Spanish wars for his ideas of freedom, and became one of the world's most accomplished and renowned guerrillas. Brooklyn with self-acquired learning. A man of profound depth of feeling and sensitivity, an exquisite sense of justice.

Sergeant Milt Felsen: The fighting Jew, who loathes all sham and loves freedom. An idealist like Goff, who fought in the same wars and on the same side, and with the same bravery. This is a Jew at his best, clever and fine and subtle, and witty.

Sergeant Lassowsky: I knew him least of all. But what goes for Goff and Milt goes for him as well, in less spectacular way perhaps. But a man of complete confidence.

Captain Robert: Thirty years old, too old for this racket, as I at thirty-eight so keenly feel. An old timer in the SOE, and a complete fanatic. His wife is a schoolteacher, and they have adopted many children. He is Canadian—part French, part Gaelic Scots. He is as square and solid and tough as nails. He had twenty-seven relatives killed in the last war and has personally killed only three Germans. He has twenty-four to go, and he will get them. He is a first-class soldier and a complete berserk. Nothing on God's earth can stop him save lead and steel. And he, too, has fought guerrilla before; this is his sixth campaign. "Only one I fought for conviction, that for France, because I am a Catholic."

[92]

A curious man to lead Loyalists, and he hopes they will not find out which side he was on.

Lieutenant Alexander Robertson: A small, wiry Scots youth with a burr you could cut with a knife. A sly smile, slightly shy, and as wild as the rest in a quiet way. A very expert man at demolition. Canny and self-reliant and completely fearless. He and Robert should get through where Quiney might get trapped.

Lieutenant Richard Crosby: Of Danvers, Massachusetts. What we Yankees like to think about when we indulge in the luxury of being proud of our ancestry. The true Revolutionary type. Keenly intelligent, sober of judgment, quick of wit. A scholar and a man of decision. He has the makings of the perfect executive, the perfect leader, despite his years and inferior rank. Physically less endowed than men like Sage and Robert and Quiney, but mentally far their superior. He should be promoted at once.

Lieutenant Colonel Anstruthers: Here we deal with the one difficult personality to describe. A brilliant man (only thirty-eight) who has let his body go to seed, for he is very fond of fine foods and wines and lives in the mind. A glandular case who goes to sleep in conferences, but who has an extremely subtle sense of humor which is sometimes cruel in an almost feminine way. He has never visited the outposts of his realm nor exposed himself to any personal danger other than through his erratic driving of automobiles. He is very intelligent and very quick. He has a very difficult job in handling the army on the one hand and his men on the other. He lacks grace and when he gives an order which seems disagreeable, fails to explain why. A little tact would make him more popular, but this lack of tact seems to be the result of shyness; he is honest and lucid but wholly theoretical. He would like to be liked but does not know the way. He cannot handle the epic personalities under him nor can he assist them in the planning of details. A scholar and a soldier on paper, and a sincere individual, wrongly placed.

Lieutenant Colonel Young: The Gael of the Heroic Age. A

huge, husky, Palaeolithic survivor of a Scot, kilted and bagpipe playing, full of clans and septs and canny judgment. Tough as nails and brave as Finn MacCool. Wise in the handling of men, a disbeliever in evolution, and as clever in human relations as he is naive in books. When he appears doubts allay, confidence returns, for he is the perfect leader of men in battle. A man to follow to hell and damnation, with the pipes skirling.

Now that the dramatic persons are in line, we shall proceed with the events of the first week of the southern campaign and the role of OSS/SOE in it.

Tuesday, February 9. On this day General Gubbins, Lieutenant Colonel Young, Avril (Young's chauffeur), and I visited Tebessa. On the way down General Gubbins drove his car with Young as passenger, and Avril drove my Studebaker with me as passenger. We proceeded to II Corps headquarters where we encountered Lieutenant Colonel Akers, a coarse, red-haired, snub-nosed individual who greeted General Gubbins as Colonel. He then introduced both me and Young as colonels. We were all colonels together; Akers exclaimed with oaths and obscenities that he hoped we were not from OSS; they had sent down a bastard named Bourgoin who had messed things up in general. Colonel Darney was at the mess. We went to the mess and ate with Colonel Darney and others. Colonel Darney was fortunately far different from Akers. We returned with Darney to the G-3 tent where we discussed problems in general and I got the story from documents on the Bourgoin case which I have since transmitted to Colonel Eddy. General Gubbins and Colonel Young explained our role to Colonel Darney, who was most understanding and helpful. We showed him our explosive turds and stones, in which he was greatly interested. Quiney (Quinney to Akers) had already been down and made a good impression. So it was arranged that we were to come down, camp, and cooperate with Corps.

Wednesday, February 10. Nothing vital to the south. I train

Ali; Quiney and Sage depart for the south. They return after Sage drives his car over a banking.

Thursday, February 11. After a snowy passage, Rossmiller, Ali, and I arrive at Pig Hill late at night. Sage, Quiney, Robertson, Robert, and the Spaniards again depart for the south. They pass Tebessa and the Tebessa gap, camp in the pine forest in the region beyond the Tebessa gap, the second patch of forest beyond Tebessa and beyond the five-mile stretch of Messerschmitt moorland.

Friday, February 12. On this day I busied myself at Pig Hill, Suk el Khemis, and Bulla Regia, getting my Studebaker fixed, getting new tires, and getting cloth, tea, and sugar for Arabs. I saw Colonel Allen and Major Haydon, and determined that from Monday on I could get Arab supplies from Haydon at Maktar, where he would then be established. Colonel Young and Major Michael Crosby were at Pig Hill; Hamish Torrance was in the hospital where Colonel Young and I visited him; Young was to take him to Guelma the following day via Tabarka and LaGalle, to visit Johnny Warren en route. Meanwhile Quiney, Sage, and company proceeded to camp number two known as Camp Cactus, where they established themselves in a cactus patch some 5 km. west of Sbeitla overlooking the town. They must have worked hard on that camp for it was very well camouflaged.

Saturday, February 13. I proceeded alone from Pig Hill via le Kef to Tebessa, where I met Sergeant Byzek, raided the QM stores for clothing and equipment, stopped at Thelepte for gasoline, and went on to Camp Cactus, arriving about dusk. Sage had been to Sidi Bou Zid to see General McQuillan, and was to establish a second and separate camp there near MacMillan, which was considered advantageous owing to the proximity of the spot to the front. Quiney and I were to continue on at Camp Cactus.

Sunday, February 14. Quiney, Sage, Byzek and I proceeded to Sheitla, en route to Sidi Bou Zid to lunch with General McQuillan. At Sheitla we stopped to have my Studebaker fixed and to load up with water for Camp Cactus. We found out that my car could not be fixed there, and also that the Germans had burst through in two places and had cut off McQuillan's headquarters. We found this out only casually by conversation, otherwise we would have blundered right into the enemy. We went back to Camp Cactus and watched the battle from the hill, great clouds of dust as the tanks roared across the plain, five Stukas dive-bombing one of the artillery batteries and taking it out about 4 km. below us, a Messerschmitt machine-gunning the road and getting one jeep and one passenger car with drivers of both. We ducked constantly into the cactus at alerts and got our hands full of spines.

The day was filled with visits to various headquarters, mainly to G-2 and G-3, which were just across the road in the far pasture. Down in front of us was parked the first armored division, subsequently lost and found again. Jerry went to see a Colonel Howze, who said that if we boys wanted to do something we could go down front and sit in foxholes and toss petard grenades and Molotov cocktails at the German heavy tanks as they rolled over us. He said he would talk it over. He did and we didn't want to. It was not OSS work. Then I went over to see if we could get a telephone laid on to keep us up on affairs; the telephone man came, and when he found we had no instrument, refused to play. Then Jerry and Quiney went to G-3 and said we did not want to toss petards; the G-3 colonel said: All right, then you can do one of two things; go far behind the lines, well behind the ridge from which the Germans advanced on Sidi Bou Zid, to take out tanks; or go up and check their advance on the right flank to the southeast of Foriana and Sbeitla. He did not know where these tanks were going or what route they would take. Quiney and Sage came home and called me, Robert, Robertson, and the sergeants into consultation. We agreed that Plan A was pure suicide without results. Plan B unfeasible because of its vagueness, and that both were beyond our powers. Jerry was very loath to give in and so was Quiney, while I was the chief exponent of refusal. Quiney backed me before Jerry did. The sergeants backed me, which finally turned Jerry. I wanted to retire to a better position to see how things went before we started to operate; Quiney wanted to take all of us into a range of barren hills to the east, to hide out and let the Germans go by. He was obsessed with this idea. So was Robert; Jerry backed me in rejecting it. Such a party could carry food and water, in addition to explosives, for less than forty-eight hours, and we would get caught as soon as we came down for water. It did not make sense. Even Robert finally admitted this. Robertson did not say much; he was game for anything.

Quiney and Sage went to G-2, G-3, and talked with Colonel Howze, who was distraught. When they said we had rejected his ideas he said: "All right, I will turn you over to Colonel _____ [I forget the name] to take part of our defensive line." "Defensive line?" said Quiney with an uplift to his voice. Howze showed temper, turned on his heel, and said: "Goodnight, there is nothing further to be done," and departed.

Quiney and Sage came back to camp feeling badly slapped. Both were extremely chagrined. We decided to shift camp backwards, and did so, to camp number three, just in front of number one, where we entered a meadow with woods on either side and camped under the pines. This was a good way from Camp Cactus, past Kasserine and Thelepte, and behind the first ridge facing the plain.

Monday, February 15. The chagrin persisted, and Quiney and I started off for Guelma. I drove my Studebaker as far as the Tebessa airport, where it ceased to run and I left it in charge of an anti-aircraft battery, well out of the way of pillagers. Then I joined Quiney and we went on to Guelma arriving about 4 p.m. We saw Anstruthers and Young, and Anstruthers took down a statement. They both felt we should have reported to Corps and should get back at once. Colonel Young asked: "Should I come?" I winked over Quiney's shoulder, knowing that only Young could fix matters. We ate quickly and left, arriving at Corps after midnight.

[97   ]

Quiney and Young saw Colonel Hewitt and all was okay; we were to keep in touch with them daily at 10 a.m. and arrange our activities. Then we went to camp, couldn't find it because it had been shifted, and I slept under a tree while Young and Avril slept in Young's car and Quiney kept searching until 3 a.m. when he found the camp, came back, and slept near us.

Tuesday, February 16. We found the camp across the meadow, well concealed, and learned that Sage had been to McQuillan's headquarters the previous day on a motorcycle, and McQuillan had expressed gratitude that he had visited him. Young, Quiney, and I went on a tour, visiting Foriana, Kasserine and Sbeitla. At all these places Young and Quiney saw officials while I did not. At Kasserine I visited the Suk and laid plans for cloth, etcetera, to lay on with Haydon for Tuesday, the 23rd. Then we returned to camp, and Quiney and Young visited Corps, while I stayed behind fixing the tent. Young went on back to Guelma. That night all of us officers played poker, using shells for chips.

Wednesday, February 17. We got up at 7:30 to find the Signal Corps outfit across the meadow departed. Byzek came in from a motorcycle trip announcing that the Germans were advancing some twelve miles east; we had heard many planes go over, and saw still more, all of them American, and we heard rifle and machine-gun firing beyond the ridge. We packed up and moved down to Corps, where Sage and I searched for a campsite across the road; Quiney went up to Corps, and returned, announcing that the plans were all made. I asked: "What are they?" and he answered: "Ask Sage, I have no time to talk," and Sage said: "To go back to camp number one and toss petards at tanks." I asked if Colonel Darney or Colonel Hewitt had ordered this. Neither had; both were absent; Quiney had proposed it as his own idea to a third colonel and been accepted.

Neither Sage nor I liked this, but there was little choice; Quiney had stayed behind, and we took the outfit to camp number one where we parked next to a group of Derbyshire Yeomenry.

They had been trapped south of Gafsa when the Germans had entered but had ridden around the town and out. They were to move on at 2:30 p.m. There was nothing between us and two panzer divisions of heavy tanks but a few Rangers with tommy guns and a few French artillerymen with ancient material. Quiney as usual was obsessed with the idea of letting the Germans roll by. He had appeared, and I got his consent to send Young a wire to come down, which the latter had stated he wanted to do before my action. I was to wait at Corps to meet him. I spent the afternoon putting detonators in the turds and stones, and disguising the dot holes; Robertson et al. in priming plastic petards. We saw outfit after outfit roll westward by.

Quiney took two patrols, one himself and one under Robert. The target was the group of sixty or seventy vehicles which G-2 had spotted at Thelepte. The three sergeants were under him. When Goff wanted to talk it over and plan things, he said: "These are orders. If you do not obey you will be courtmartialed." I did not know this until the next day.

Sage and I went to Corps, he to tell what they were doing, and I to wait for Colonel Young. I ate in the mess and then waited in the liaison tent with a tank corps officer who told me about the loss of 100 Mark 3 and Mark 4 tanks. Then Colonel Huntington (not our colonel of that name) called me over to G-3, and said Brigadier McNab wanted to bomb Thelepte; where were our men? I said they were heading for there, so he called off the bombing. After midnight Colonel Young appeared and went with me to the camp.

Thursday, February 18. At the camp Colonel Young decided that our position was untenable, and ordered us to move to near Corps. Quiney who had just returned, protested, but to no avail. Quiney had led his patrols to 3 km. of Thelepte, seen nothing, decided the men were tired, and returned with no results. We went back; Young told Corps what had happened, and to go ahead and bomb if there was still time. Young and I were to meet

[99]

the rest at the pass in front of the first ridge outside Tebassa where we had a gun position (one gun). The men did not show up for a long time. Finally some came, and Robertson and I went ahead to find a camp. Everything was taken and it took a long while. Also, the Austin PU in which we were riding was very feeble. Also, Sage's Renault had developed a broken driving shaft and was still at camp number three. When Robertson and I returned we found that one of our 2½-ton trucks had been sideswiped by a tank trailer, capsizing it, and injuring three Spaniards, one perhaps fatally, as well as destroying the truck. An ambulance took the three Spaniards off and another truck brought the men. We got camped just as the troops next us were blowing reveille. I got one-and-a half-hours sleep, Colonel Young none.

The rest of that day we spent on the alert to move if so indicated. Many councils were held and expeditions sent. Jerry and Drake (Sage's colored driver) went to Ain Beidha to get a new truck and Drake was lost coming back until after 4:30. A British driver went after the oil pump of the wrecked truck and came back with the announcement that his prize was broken. And finally Sage kept saying that he wanted (a) to get the tarpaulin from the truck, and (b) tow in his Renault to keep the Germans from getting it. Colonel Young kept refusing these suggestions, but finally Jerry went after the tarpaulin. It is my impression that Colonel Young, after many refusals, finally said: "All right, God damn it, go get it if you must, but come right back," but I may be wrong. In view of Sage's failure to return I do not like to trust my memory on this point. At any rate Sage took Byzek about 4:30 to 5 and did not come back.

Quiney insisted on going behind, so at my suggestion this was on a volunteer basis, after Colonel Young had agreed that he could go behind. He asked the Spaniards by groups; two voted to go and one to stay. Sage was absent from these deliberations. Quiney, Robert, Robertson, and twenty Spaniards, including the two doctors, were to go, and they packed supplies and explosives and made ready to leave in a separate truck that was to take them as far as possible. The rest, under Sage (if he returned) were to go on to Djebel Kouif to open a camp. Young had brought Richard Crosby down to relieve me, and in Sage's absence Crosby was to take charge of the outside group. When Sage failed to come by 7 p.m. we started, passed through Tebessa, and got the convoy on the road to Djebel Kouif, after bucking tanks in the dark coming down from Le Kef. It was extremely hazardous driving. Then Colonel Young left Crosby and party (Quiney's car had cracked on the way), and he, I, and Avril went back to Guelma, arriving about 2 a.m. Crosby was to send out a search patrol after Sage and Byzek if they failed to show up at Djebel Kouif by morning. At Guelma I went to bed for a few hours sleep and in the morning greeted Charles Mackintosh, who was to go to Djebel Kouif with Colonel Young after lunch. I proceeded to Algiers under Colonel Young's orders to rest, arrived at 11:30 p.m. after driving all day without food, reported to Colonel Eddy when he got up in the morning, and the next day went to a clinic where I was ordered into a hospital for ten days. I refused, but have been in bed in Villa Rose ever since.

C. S. Coon

Feb. 23, 1943, Villa Rose, Algiers

SECOND INTERIM

THIS period can be covered very briefly. After I arrived in Algiers, I went to a hospital to get some vitamin A tablets for night blindness, and the army doctor ordered me to stay there in bed in complete seclusion, except that I could see friends for one hour a day. I refused, and went back to Villa Rose. Colonel Eddy then went to Tunisia for a week to visit the front, with Colonel Ellery Huntington and Assistant Secretary of War Mr. McCloy; Colonel Eddy left me in his bed for this period, and there I was well taken care

[101]

of by Lucina, Colonel Eddy's cook, and other members of his staff. Old friends, such as Captain Movius of the Air Corps, Colonel Brian Clark, Colonel Rattay, and Colonel Sharp of G-2, came to visit me, and I wrote up Part IV, which appears in the preceding section of this report.

Colonel Eddy returned and said that Colonel Young was anxious for me to return to Tunisia, but Dr. Rossmiller refused to give his professional approval. Thereupon Colonel Eddy ordered me back to Morocco to rest. I went there via Oran and Gibraltar, arriving in Tangier on March 5. I stayed there five days, and proceeded to Casablanca and Oujda with Gordon Browne.

CHAPTER FIVE

The Spanish Border

Historical Setting: March to May 1943

THE last narrative section returns to the Spanish border and the Riffians, Coon's first love. On the fighting front in Tunisia the Allies shook off the effects of Kasserine and whipsawed the Axis armies east and west. General Omar Bradley secretly took command of II Corps to release Patton for the preparation already under way for the invasion of Sicily. Finally, on May 8, under assault from the American II Corps and the British First and Eighth Armies, von Arnim surrendered and the campaign for North Africa was over.

In the West, meanwhile, as all this was moving to a conclusion, General Mark Clark and his colleagues continued to express concern about the danger of an invasion from Spanish territory. It is hard to guess whether they were serious about this. Perhaps so. Or they may have regarded the threat as a useful doctrine for a rear area and used it to maintain vigilance against the real dangers of infiltration, assassination, and sabotage.

There was, however, another aspect of the Spanish idea that is easy to underestimate at this distance. The very word *Spain* produced powerful emotional responses in almost everyone in those days. The Spanish Civil War was a very recent event. To some,

Spain was the crucible of black magic in which the present war was formed. To others it was sacred and tragic ground where the Republic had died. All these reactions, of whatever kind, came in large sizes, creating symbols and myths. Spain was strong medicine.

Completely unconnected with anything that Coon was doing, and for the most part after he had left Morocco, the OSS fell into that Spanish trap. Another OSS officer, acting on his own authority, it is said, his head presumably filled exclusively with ideological purity, decided that it was more important to start the Spanish Civil War all over again than to keep Spain neutral. Under the code name Banana, he launched an operation to see what he could stir up. He sent in a contingent of Spanish radicals equipped with American arms, American code books, and American transmitters. They came to ugly and inglorious grief, incriminated hundreds of others, and left plain evidence linking the United States with armed subversion in Spain. Ambassador Carlton Hays in Madrid lied stoutly in defense of his country's innocence, but he also made such a row in Washington that OSS activities in Spain were severely curtailed and almost stopped. The OSS rated Operation Banana as its worst blunder of the war.

In this final period, Coon's main activity, as many of the details of his narrative indicate, was intelligence gathering once again, notwithstanding his fascination with Germans across the border. He kept track of the Spanish and German orders of battle, the status of garrisons and fortifications, and the movements of Germans in Spanish territory. For this he used native sources in large part, but clearly not entirely. He kept watch on the Vichy officials and the Axis agents they frequently protected.

Then there are the occasional scenes. Reading these vivid, sharp vignettes today, one is struck not only by their prophetic quality but by the close-range reality of the social and political conditions in which they occur. Other men could see these things from a distance with less distinct resolution. Roosevelt did and his awareness underlay a continuing friction with Churchill, who, perhaps equally aware, chose to defy the future. (*I did not become His Majesty's First Minister to preside over the liquidation of the empire.*) Coon's kind of perception, however, undecorated by political rhetoric, was rare. Its accuracy was demonstrated as early as 1945 by the serious rising of Moslem radical nationalists under Massali Hajj. The deluge was not long in coming.

Toymakers and Saboteurs

ON March 5 I found Browne in bed in Tangier, with his old pleurisy, and I went to bed likewise, because the trip from Algiers had worn out what little strength I had regained. However, in a few days we were both up and about, and he wanted to go to Casablanca to see Colonel Lambert who had taken Colonel Rattay's place as the man interested in our Riffian organization and that of Mr. Strings.

So I went with him, and we drove down to Casa in the Plymouth, one of the two cars belonging to Colonel Eddy's office. Browne's Chevrolet was at Casa awaiting new wheels, and my Studebaker was still at Tebessa. We found only General Wilson at Casa, and proceeded to Rabat, but not before both of us had been hauled in to have a conference with Brigadier General Strong (British) who was on his way to Algiers to take over G-2. He was apparently an SIS man. He wanted to know all about channels of communicating intelligence in the North African theater, and we told him all we were able.

At Rabat we saw General Keyes, who said that Colonel Lambert had gone to the front, and also General Wilbur. General Keyes called Oujda and talked with General Clark, who said he wanted to see Browne and me, and General Wilbur then proposed to take us the next day to Oujda in his private plane. So we returned to Casa, and the next day General Wilbur picked us up there at the airport, and we proceeded to Oujda, taking a close view of the ruins of Volubilis, which interested General Wilbur, on the way.

We were put off for a couple of days, and finally saw Colonel Howard (AC of S, G-2) whom Browne had known at Oran; Colonel Kenmore (AC of S, G-3), General Grunther, and General Clark. These officers were much interested in our Spanish Zone subversive activities, and encouraged us to draw up new plans involving the invasion of the Spanish Zone overland, and to keep our native leaders interested. General Clark instructed Browne to return to Tangier for this purpose, and me to remain in Oujda and vicinity attached to Colonel Howard's staff, as long as the threat through Spain and the Spanish Zone lasted. It was agreed that this threat would be over with the fall of Tunis to the Allied forces, and that is why I was released by Colonel Howard on May 8, 1943.

After Browne and I had seen General Clark we returned by plane to Casablanca. I had to go back there because I had brought no clothing with me, having expected to be in Oujda only twenty-four hours at the most. From Casa, Browne and I proceeded to Fez; there I waited for our British colleage Stripes, whom General Clark wanted to see; Browne proceeded to his post via Casa. Stripes and I traveled to Oujda by army car; after a couple of days General Clark saw him, and Stripes explained his plans for impeding the Spanish and German war effort in case they should start a Moroccan offensive. As always there was complete agreement between OSS and SOE, and the army approved the plans of both. Stripes was to take out the European population and sow discord in the Spanish Army, while we were to have the natives. Among other things Stripes had it all laid out to let loose two hives of bees in the Spanish HQ at H hour D day, which would tie up the Spanish staff work effectively for at least a vital half hour, since the building is full of interconnecting doors that are always open, and is protected by screens.

When Stripes left, I was faced with a period of waiting, and attempted to find some cover job to occupy myself with. It seemed most useful for me to learn the Spanish Moroccan border, or at least the eastern end of it, as thoroughly as possible, to learn what was going on in that mysterious and feverish city, Melilla, and to work on the problem of enemy intelligence and sabotage directed at our area.

At first I obtained vehicles from the Fifth Army, and drove over all the roads and trails along the Moulouya bank from the mouth of the Moulouya to a point south of the International Bridge where ordinary cars could not pass. I took with me two CIC men, Nicholas Cokenias and George Farah, being respectively a Greek and an Arabic-speaking Syrian. They were very intelligent men, and I enjoyed their company very much.

After about a week Colonel Parsons, the head of the CIC, arrived from Casablanca, and with him Captain Bourgoin, a Frenchman who ran a garage at Casablanca and who had been of great value to King and Reid before the landing. He was French liaison to G-2 of the Fifth Army, a position that Colonel Parsons had obtained for him. Sometimes he wore French uniform, sometimes civilian clothes (or as he said, clotheses). His civilian garb was worn and disreputable, since as he said the ration board would give him no bons for clothes because he was a de Gaullist. I gave him a suit of Harris tweed which my wife had sent me, and which by some miracle fitted him very well. He was not very popular with many of the other French, who looked upon him as a traitor, and he avoided and was avoided by Colonel Poidonot, the head of the French liaison section of the Fifth Army; Poidonot is a Vichyite and an ulcer in the flank of the Fifth Army. I hope that some means will be found to remove Poidonot.

Captain Bourgoin had been in Morocco nearly thirty years, and knew everybody. He had spent much of this time as agent for Morocco of the Vacuum Oil Company, and in every town and village he could dig out at a moment's notice his former agent, or someone to whom he had once loaned some vast sum of money. Hence everywhere we went we were sure of a free meal and much local information.

Sometimes we went in jeeps, sometimes in command cars; sometimes in Citroens, Peugeots, or Buicks. Wherever we went the captain, who was an amateur racing driver, insisted on driving, and one time we raced to Casablanca in a front-wheel-drive Citroen at 120 km. per hour, without slowing down on the curves. I soon decided that my only means of obtaining peace of mind was to decide that Captain Bourgoin was infallible, but Colonel Parsons, who sometimes went with us, never came to that decision and as a result his nervous system was nearly shattered.

In our border foraging we crossed trails in jeeps and command cars that horses couldn't walk over. We visited sheikhs and kaids and rich Jews and French farmers and garage keepers and army officers and cartographic surveyors and customs officers and smugglers and border *passeurs* and *chefs de poste* and practically everyone else from Guerçif to the mouths of the Moulouya.

We also had close relations in Oujda with three Frenchmen: Captain Bachelot, head of the local DAP (Administration Politique) M. Violle, the local police head, and Captain Legrand (His real name Lefort) head of the 5me Bureau, corresponding to the OSS. All were on our side and passionately anti-Vichy; all but Legrand were constantly in hot water with the Nogues-Guillaume-Bouyassi administration. Bachelot was reprimanded and fired for giving information to the Americans (actually to Lieutenant Kline of G-2; they did not know he gave it to us). Violle was about to resign when we left because all his arrests were thwarted. Legrand, who looks like Lil'l Abner and who drowns, poisons, and shoots his victims at will, was left alone, which was perhaps healthier for the officials concerned. I would not like to be on his bad books myself.

Violle was about to resign for the following reason: he had arrested some thirty-odd enemy agents, all Moslems sent across by Spaniards and Germans in Melilla, during the last four months. In due process of law he had to send them to Meknes to the Military Tribunal. There they were supposed to be tried and sentenced. I have not the exact figures, but almost all that he had sent were let free, and he was reprimanded for using "American police methods." I do not doubt that he occasionally used such methods, for I once heard a Spanish sergeant screaming in his back office; he had caught the sergeant exchanging notes with a Moor from Oran in a deserted farm on the French side of the border.

However, hard times breed hard methods, and if anyone was ever to break up the Melilla spy ring it was necessary to put the fear of God into the enemy agents. What finally enraged Violle was a case in which he arrested a notorious Riffian spy on his way from Oran to Melilla with a document sewn in the leather of his scrip. This document was a complete record of all shipping in Oran harbor over a period of ten days, immediately preceding. Violle sent the culprit and the document to Meknes, and the culprit was remanded for further hearing "when Violle could get more and better evidence." Despite the fact that the document was a form issued by Kraemer in Melilla, with which we were already familiar, the court stated that "Capt. Bachelot planted this document on the accused in order to revenge himself on him." This was not very pleasant for Captain Bachelot either.

It seems that in Meknes the court interpreter and the defense lawyer were the parents of a young husband and wife; they distorted the evidence and got their clients off, at the price of a hearty fee from Kraemer. Thus the Meknes court defeated all the attempts of honest officials in Oujda to prevent enemy activity in the Oujda-Oran area. I will never forget a speech Violle made to me on the subject of American negligence, how we would lose all we had won and more if we let the good Frenchmen who supported us be kicked around while we honored the Vichyites and pro-Axis excrements who kicked them. This speech had a double effect on me since (a) it was true and (b) I could understand him; Violle was the only one of the three who worked with us whom I could understand; Bachelot and Legrand both talked out of the sides of their mouths while clutching cigarettes with their lips, and used slang of a complication which defeated my efforts to decipher it. Even Bourgoin had trouble understanding Bachelot.

One place we were always pleased to visit was the Dubois farm. About ten miles north of Taourirt a Breton named Legrand, some eleven years before, had drawn off water from the Wed Za, and created an oasis in the midst of utter desert. Here he had built up with his own hands a little kingdom lined with shade trees, rich with grain, clover, fruit trees, vegetable gardens, and pasture; here clean sows dragged their bellies on the ground while they grazed off clover with the cattle. I would not believe that pigs would graze until I saw this. He also had his own machine shop, his lighting plant, and everything needed to make his realm self-contained.

Dubois had three men working for him who interested us. One was an old and fleet-footed Riffian named Moktar, who trotted back and forth between the farm and Nador (outside Melilla) where he had a brother who was a policeman. He carried messages back and forth, and obtained information about the Spaniards from his brother. The other two were a couple of Spaniards who had escaped from the Spanish Zone and were working in Dubois's machine shop. They kept up a regular correspondence by letter with friends in Melilla. Sometimes Moktar carried these letters, sometimes others. Every time Captain Bourgoin and I would visit Dubois, these two Spaniards would show us their lat est letters. Thus Dubois maintained a private intelligence service which was of considerable use to us.

Another man who had a private service was Jacques Choucroune of Berkane, whom we also visited regularly. He owns seven farms in the Beni Znassen country, including one right on the river; across the river from his farm the Spanish telephone and telegraph line runs, and we had planned to swim across and tap it nighttimes when the river should abate enough. Choucroune had a gang of Riffians who regularly swam it and delivered information. He was also prepared to pass people. Whenever he heard something particularly interesting he called us on the phone and we visited him.

Still a third man who ran a private service was Jose Pascual, a Catalan, a cook by trade, who has a private grudge against Franco and wants his revenge. Jose runs a canteen at the railroad station of Taourirt; while the thirtieth infantry was camped there he made a lot of money selling smuggled Spanish brandy; he was going to get me 100 bottles, but was unable to before my departure. With the 100 bottles I could have "made friends and influenced people" more than in any other way. Jose was in touch with most of the smugglers of that region, and had one Riffian with gold teeth in his employ. This Riffian offered to go across the border and bring us back three complete Spanish uniforms, for men 168, 160, and 155 cm. tall respectively for 1500 pesetas. Jose could pass anyone we wanted and have them taken all the way to Melilla. Our method of communicating with him was simple; we would call the *chef des postes* at Taourirt, and gave him a code message, or Jose would have the *chef des postes* call us and tell us that our firewood was at the station. We used the living room of the *chef des postes*, who is an ardent de Gaullist, as a rendezvous place.

Another man who could pass people for us was the sheikh Hamid er Rih, or Hamid the Wind, so called because his grandfather had a horse as swift as the wind, and his family had taken the surname Rih in honor of the horse. Sheikh Wind has a house on a height overlooking the mouth of the Moulouya; his land touched on a ford, and on the other side he had a friend named Luiz, who was secretly a Spanish Loyalist. When Sheikh Wind would signal, Luiz would swim across the river, and he would carry objects or messages, or ferry people, as desired.

Two other men with whom we kept in contact were Driss Riffi, and Si Hamid Ramdani. Driss Riffi was a former general of Abd el Krim's. He was a native of the Gzennaya, the tribe which I knew best, and we knew many mutual friends among the men of that tribe. Driss acted as local boss of all the Riffians going through Oujda, and those mounted to thousands annually; for at least two generations it has been the practice of the Riffians to migrate annually to Algeria where they are hired as seasonal harvesters, reaping grain, picking grapes, and trampling wine. All of them pass through Oujda and most stop in to see Driss Riffi. In the first week of May the annual rush eastward had just begun. Hence it is obvious that Driss Riffi was in a number-one position to glean all kinds of information about the Spanish Zone and to check on possible agents the Germans might be slipping through as harvesters. Driss Riffi also had a friend who was shaush of the Spanish Consulate in Oran, and when I left he was about to get in touch with that man and put him on our payroll. This was undoubtedly done after I left by Bourgoin and Donald Downes; it was a golden opportunity to penetrate the most active enemy espionage agency in that area.

Si Hamid Ramdani was the local head of the Nationalist party. The first time I saw him I went to his house to dinner with Gordon Browne, Caho, Bourgoin, Captain Bachelot, Captain Bouilly de Barreau, and Mme. Bouilly de Barreau. Now these were a picked lot of Frenchmen from the native point of view. All of them spoke Arabic. All had been in the native affairs service. Yet they sat there and talked French to one another and ignored their host; and Si Hamid would not even have eaten with us if Gordon and I had not insisted. The Frenchmen jabbered at a great rate, while pointing chicken bones at each other for emphasis, about how many Shluh they had killed in this and that campaign, etcetera, a topic which could not have been too pleasant for an Arab nationalist. And they were among the best Frenchmen in Morocco from the native viewpoint.

Si Hamid's chief value to us lay in that he was in constant touch with Abd el Khalek Torres and his rebel Nationalist crowd in Tetuan, and he thus could let us know what they were up to. For example, he rendered a considerable service when he told us that the Germans had instructed Torres to spread the following rumor among all the natives of Morocco: At a given moment the Germans will drop paratroops behind the main road (Casa to Oran) while a gang of saboteurs from the Spanish Zone will work on transport and communication. At the same time the Germans will come through Spain, and Japs will land by submarine at Ifni.

We had already picked up parts of this from three sources and it was beginning to look as if the Germans were pretty indiscreet, when Si Hamid's revelation settled the business.

Spaniards and Germans had several services based on the Spanish Zone and several schools of espionage and sabotage, but they produced very little in the way of results. Richter, whom the Arabs call Abdullah, since he is a convert to Islam, lives at el Ksar el Kebir, and runs a mill just over the line at Araboua. In this mill he has lots of explosives, and the keys to the charges with which the el Ksar bridge is mined. Abdullah Richter runs a school, but so far his pupils have not taken any honors. In fact we could not learn of any graduates. It would be the easiest thing in the world to knock off Abdullah and blow up his mill since he is only a few yards over the border; in fact, it was rather hard to keep people from knocking him off. Captain Bourgoin would have done it at the drop of a hat, and was always thinking up better and better ways to do it; he was a great friend of the local kaid, who would do it for him, except that he wanted to do the job with his own hands; "We must show no pity to these blackguards," he said. Also, Lieutenant Colonel Parsons of the Counter-Intelligence Corps wanted to take a crack at the mill; in fact, Richter was a very popular person and his ears must have been constantly burning.

Melilla was our chief objective from Oujda. In Melilla Kraemer had an establishment on the Rua Ibanez Martin; he was the vice-consul from way back, and ran a rather plodding intelligence service, of Riffians and others filling in blanks which enumerated vehicles, ships, etcetera. The blank from Oran which we saw was potentially useful to the enemy, but one on-road count that came into Colonel Howard's hands was so inaccurate and exaggerated our material so much that General Clark told us not to prevent these agents from filling out their blanks. I have seen people jotting down numbers along the roadside and have no doubt they were doing this for a purpose; I agree with General Clark that this is not very dangerous.

It seems particularly futile to try to keep this kind of information from the enemy when all the Spanish consul has to do is to ride along the Rabat-Meknes road through the forest of Marmora; there the I Armored Corps has beautiful hand-painted signs on trees and posts all along, telling the traveler where the tanks are, where the hospital is, where the supply dumps are, and where the mine and booby-trap school is. All the agent needs is to be able to copy what he sees; he does not even need to know English.

Much more interesting to us than Kraemer and his gang was a mysterious man, tall, thickset, and very blond, who ran a demolition school in Rua Ysabella Catolica; he called himself Emilio Darrio, or Carlos; Downes identified him with Karl Frick, alias Carlos Frique, alias Harry Wood, who pulled off the Black Tom job in the last war. He is the German vice-consul at Cartagena, and spends his time between that city and Melilla. Captain Bourgoin swore by all his gods that he would get this prince of all blackguards, and on one occasion we seemed in a fair way to do this.

Two Germans made a date with the Kaid Mansouri of the Beni Znassen to meet on an island of the Moulouya. Now Kaid Mansouri was an Axis sympathizer, and for months we had wondered how Nogues had the temerity to protect him. Finally, however, Nogues sent an order to Legrand to cook up an excuse to arrest the kaid, and grab him. But we wanted to get Frick at the same time, since the chances were that Frick would be one of the Germans.

At a certain spot along the Moulouya, the river once took a couple of hairpin bends, so that an area a kilometer long and half as wide projected from the Spanish Zone into French territory, with an isthmus only a few yards wide separating the two bends of the river. A few years back the river changed its course; this gap was flooded, and the bends dried, so that this "island" was connected by dry land with the French Zone, and was separated from the rest of the Spanish Zone by water. Still this piece of land remained Spanish territory. Now the Germans were to meet Mansouri on this "island"; the Germans would have to swim, while Mansouri could ride to the rendezvous on his horse.

We laid elaborate plans to capture or kill the Germans, and presented these to General Clark; he said that we could not step foot on Spanish territory, nor shoot over it; we would have to get the Germans onto French territory before we could touch them. Colonel Parsons, Captain Bourgoin, Legrand, Captain Bachelot, and I were to pull the job. But unfortunately, a few days before the meeting was to take place, Kaid Mansouri collapsed in the street in Berkane, and had to be carried home, where he lay in a coma. He has probably, by now, died. It was my belief and that of Captain Bourgoin that Legrand had had him poisoned, but we cannot prove this. At any rate the kaid's illness prevented our carrying out this very interesting operation. It also saved Frick (if it was to be Frick) some painful moments, for Captain Bourgoin

on the subject before we gave up. Eventually he came through.

On the whole the enemy sabotage effort, which seemed impressive with their schools at Melilla, Alcazar, Tetuan, and Tangier, amounted to zero. Now that Tunis has fallen and the Fifth Army is no longer a skeleton, and now that we no longer have to handle Spain with sugar tongs, it should be possible to exert pressure on the Spaniards to root these "blackguards" out. In fact, the Boston *Herald* of June 4 states that the British have already put in an opening wedge by protesting about enemy activity in Tangier.

Speaking of Spaniards, I must confess that I do not feel competent to handle these little people, whom the Riffians call "Buzharwans," or the Fathers of Bullfrogs. Bourgoin and I always called them Buzharwans when conversing, and the use of this and other code words made our conversation incomprehensible to others, since we usually talked a mixture of English, French, and Arabic. A code language was necessary when we were being driven around by an army driver in a command car or jeep (the army wouldn't let us take a vehicle without a driver).

The Spaniards always seem to me like a separate biological creation. They are small, sternly chiseled men, intent on their own interests and with ideals and preoccupations that I cannot easily understand. They have to have certain things, like cigarettes and cinemas, and they are afraid of things that seem inconsequential to us, while they are brave in unexpected ways. They have no regard for other civilizations or other peoples, but continue on their way like busy ants intent on moving pieces of straw across a sidewalk where human beings are walking. And they insist on making their lives as complicated as possible with seven kinds of identity cards, certificates of inutility, tintype photographs, and by stopping each other every half kilometer to copy all these things down. It is not just Fascism that does this; all kinds of Spaniards do it and consider these actions somehow necessary. When they stopped me and followed me and generally made a great ceremony of inspecting and checking and watching me, I thought at first that it was a campaign of nerves, to annoy me, but I soon discovered that they were paying me a compliment, and they were always very polite. Once at Sheshawen I remember, when Browne and I stepped out of our car, an official came up and bowed and asked us to enter the police station, where he announced rapidly before we could say anything: "You are Señor Gordon Harris Brownie, vice-consul of the United States of America, and you are Señor Carleton Stevens Coon, special assistant of the Legation of the United States of America"; then he wiped the sweat off his brow and smiled nervously, like a child who has just spoken a piece and wishes to be complimented. We bowed and he bowed, and we went out and sat in a café.

My first dealings with Spaniards in Oujda were not happy, nor were my second. It seems that Downes, before going to London, had sent three men, of whom the leader was one Gomez, to Oujda, where they were supposed to cross over to Melilla, or at least pave the way for such a crossing. He told me about this before he left (I was visiting Algiers at the time) and how I could get in touch with them. I arrived in Oujda and found G-2 in an uproar; these three little men had appeared in Colonel Howard's office and demanded pistols, bicycles, and money. Colonel Parsons, who was present, had enough sense to realize that there might be more in this than met the eye, and he ushered them out and made a date for them to come to his room in the Majestic, and then asked us to be there.

The three arrived as scheduled, and stood there perspiring. Gomez, a scholarly looking man in thick spectacles, started talking about Ricardo (Corporal Sickler), and I at once realized that these were Downes's men. So I gave them some money and told them to say nothing and do nothing until further notice. Then I called Algiers on the phone and asked Ricardo to come down at once, which he did, and he paid off these men and told them to go away.

Then Ricardo brought down three more men; they had to have a hideout. So Bourgoin and I arranged with Jack Chouoroune to put them on one of his farms where they would act as orange-tree pruners until we could get them their papers and clothes; Choucroune had a lot of dead and partly dead trees, owing to a failure of his irrigation system. We got them eighteen blankets and many boxes of food from the Quartermasters, and fixed them a room at the farm. Bourgoin put a Jew named Bordier in charge of them.

Bordier needs a word of comment. I do not know his real name, but Bourgoin had to make up a non-Semitic name for him, so with his peculiar sense of humor, he named him Bordier, which means brothel-keeper in old French. Bordier does not know Old French and thinks this is a fine name. Our code name for Bordier is Mr. Whorehouse. He hangs around cafés waiting for Bourgoin to give him jobs to do; Bourgoin called the cafés "Mr. Whorehouse's offices."

Bordier and Ricardo took the three men out to the farm at night; I did not go because there was no room in the car. The three men took one look at the place and refused to stay. They saw a Riffian there and were frightened; Spaniards are almost all afraid of Riffians. The Riffian is an old man who has worked for Jack Choucroune for thirty years.

So Bordier took them into town and lodged them with a Jewish family; Bourgoin and I started looking for Tercio (Spanish Foreign Legion) uniforms for them to wear when they should cross the border. This search took us from Casablanca to Sidi Bel Abbes and occupied five days. Then they announced that they wanted not Tercio but Regulares uniforms; so the search began anew.

Meanwhile they wanted cigarettes, a checkerboard, and Spanish playing cards, the kind with intestines and kidneys on them instead of pips and numbers. One day I went to see them and they were out; they had all gone to the movies. Once when I was on the uniform search one of them came down with an attack of malaria, and Gomez, of gang number one, who was supposed to have gone away, came to Colonel Parsons in high excitement, and Colonel Parsons got the man an army doctor. We got the sick man atebrine, but he refused to take it; he had to have quinine injections; Spaniards apparently have to take all medicine by the needle.

Meanwhile, also, the Jewish family had eaten up all the provisions we had drawn for the Spaniards, and they were wandering around the streets; Ricardo, who had gone back to Oran, had to be sent for once more, and he had to take them away.

I confess that it was partly my fault, and partly Bordier's. Bourgoin fired Bordier and sent him to Fez to be out of the way. Downes, having returned from London, came to Oujda to run the Spanish show personally, and after his arrival all seemed to go well. Downes and Ricardo can handle Spaniards; I cannot.

When I left Oujda on May 9, Downes and Bourgoin were in charge. They were to keep up the connections Bourgoin and I had started, and Downes was to handle the infiltration of Melilla, and Spain, from Oujda. Downes was very popular with Colonel Howard and Colonel Parsons and all of the CIC crowd; I am sure that he will do a good job and will keep up the cordial relations between the OSS and the Fifth Army.

When I left Colonel Howard handed me a document, which I copy:

HEADQUARTERS FIFTH ARMY
A.P.O. 3464 U.S. Army

9 May 1943

SUBJECT: Commendation
TO: Dr. Carl Coon

1. I wish to congratulate and commend you for the most effective manner with which you have performed your duties as special assistant to the A. C. of S., G-2, Fifth Army, for the past several months.

2. Your thorough knowledge of the North Africa Arabs, together with the energetic, loyal and conscientious performance of your duties have been of inestimable assistance to the Fifth Army.

3. I wish you every success and happiness in the future.

EDWIN B. HOWARD,
Colonel, G.S.C.,
A.C. of S., G-2

I include this not to pat myself on the back, but to illustrate that it is possible for OSS personnel to win the favor of and fit into the scheme of a regular army unit, about which I will speak more presently.

CHAPTER SIX

Observations and Conclusions

Historical Setting

IN his brief section of comment and analysis, the expression of how things appeared to him in 1943, Coon spends some time on the advantages of different kinds of cover. His experience, of course, was limited to wartime, but it is interesting that the CIA in peacetime still relies on the same kind of cover with which Coon began—diplomatic. There seems to be none other as good, particularly for station chiefs.

Recently, however, the practice has encountered unprecedented difficulties and hazards, and not exclusively from foreign powers. Americans who dislike CIA methods and performance, using internal evidence from public sources, have been identifying CIA agents under diplomatic cover and publishing their names. The perpetrators claim that this diminishes their effectiveness— which it does—without endangering their lives—which is open to question. The revelations are perfectly legal as the law now stands in this unusual country.

It is a curious state of affairs, to say the least. Many people who do not approve of blowing the cover of CIA agents would be unwilling to see legislation curtailing the freedom of speech that permits it. The dilemma is ridiculous but not trivial, and it is pe-

[123]

culiarly our own. One feels that it might have bothered the OSS less than it does the CIA.

Afterthoughts for Future Use

AT this point I would like to pass a few remarks on the role of OSS in the total war effort, both as I have observed it in action and as I feel that it should function in the future. As I understand it the OSS is a special service with specially selected and specially trained personnel, whose function it is to complement the activities of other more numerous and more overt branches of the government. It is our job to go ahead of the army and navy and lay open the ground for them; to find out things that their normal services cannot discover; to perform hostile or aggressive acts that they cannot normally accomplish. So we should be able to keep on good terms with not only our own legitimate services, but those of our allies as well, and with the underground services of the Allied governments also. This can best be illustrated by dealing with such services one by one.

Army. Technically, OSS is a part of G-3 and hence a part of the army. But the army does not always understand our rôle. When we are in a specific theater we fall technically under the orders of the commander of that theater. Thus in Tunisia the northern SOE-OSS group under Major Torrance was subject to the command of the Fifth Corps HQ. The southern group under Major Quiney was under the command of the II Corps at Tebessa. Trouble arose when a colonel of the II Corps advance HQ asked us to go out behind the Germans, sit in foxholes, and throw plastic grenades at the Mark VIs as they rolled over us. He thought that we were some kind of special suicide shock troops; he did not know that we included three of the finest guerrilla commanders of the Spanish Civil War, one university professor, a major of paratroops, and other specialists who could not easily be replaced; that we were all at least bilingual; and that our enlisted men were Spaniards ready to be sent through the lines in civilian clothes as agents.

Later on General Clark was technically the boss of Gordon Browne and myself. He, however, knew what we were trained for and gave us a free rein to work in any manner we pleased, furnishing us with vehicles, rations, personnel, and anything and anybody else within reason that we wanted. The only times that he placed any restriction on our activities were when he feared that we might create a border incident to bring about a war with Spain before we were ready for it. In the Fifth Army we were directly, however, under the AC of S of C-2, rather than G-3. Colonel Howard held in his secret files our plans for the invasion of Spanish Morocco and the arming of our native allies. Yet Colonel Robinson of G-3 did the planning, and it was he rather than Colonel Howard who decided that the time we might have used these native allies had passed, and that the reason for my attachment to the Fifth Army had ceased to exist.

For OSS personnel to be under the absolute orders of the local theater commander is fine, and a great aid to coordination of effort, *as long as the theater commander knows who we are and what we are suited to perform,* but if the theater commander does not know these facts we may waste time and effort and lose valuable personnel needlessly.

OSS personnel, like other soldiers, cannot consider themselves "unexpendable." Everyone from the President down is expendable under certain circumstances. There are times always when we must risk almost certain death, but these times differ for different people like anyone else. An OSS man should be prepared to die in the performance of his duties, and these duties are intelligence, antitransport, anticommunication, antimorale. His job is not antipersonnel, unless the personnel in question be the top of a hierarchy, like Mussolini or Hitler or Franco, or someone else in a high position whose death will cause confusion and disaster to the enemy.

Another fact about the theater commanders: They are accustomed to putting people in jobs and leaving them there indefinitely. Each time an OSS man is attached to a theater commander there must be a definite goal set, or a potential time limit, otherwise he will drag on and waste time after his job is done. In the case of my connection with the Fifth Army, the time set was the fall of Tunis, after which the threat from the Spanish border would have ceased to be important. If this limit had not been set I would still be with the Fifth Army and might even have stayed with it for the rest of the war, for they found me useful in counterintelligence, which is not my job.

I furthermore feel that even if an OSS man is attached to a theater commander, General Donovan or his representative should reserve the right to withdraw him; the man may be needed more in a new theater than in the one in which he is working, and the commander of the old theater may not understand this.

Another point which needs to be brought up, and which I will discuss further in the final section of this conclusion, is that an OSS man attached to a theater commander should have the right to wear the uniform of an officer when he wants to. Otherwise he will be constantly kicked around by sentries and MPs, he will have trouble drawing stores, PX personnel may refuse to serve him, and worst of all he will be very conspicuous. Furthermore, no OSS personnel should go under the cover of enlisted men. They are too subject to army regulations and discipline and for this reason their OSS work is liable to be at the least restricted, at the worst completely thwarted.

Ricardo Sickler's experiences in Oujda furnish an excellent example of this principle. When he arrived there he could find no place to sleep, and all that Captain Bourgoin and I could get him was a berth in an old Wagon-Lit carriage drawn up on the siding near the railroad station. To get him even this we had to confer with Sergeant Freshman who had charge of billeting. Sergeant Freshman is a notorious gossip, and this aroused his long-nosed curiosity. Once in his berth, another sergeant whose cabin he was to share came in and found him. The sergeant resented his presence, and tried to throw him out. The next night and other nights Ricardo slept in my sleeping bag on my bedroom floor. It looked very curious to have a parachute corporal sharing a civilian's quarters, in one of the three best rooms in the army dormitory in the Fifth Army Headquarters. Ricardo might as well have hung a sign about his neck, "I am a Secret Agent," and this was no fault of his. I might have hung a similar sign, being garbed as a civilian.

Another way in which OSS men can be particularly useful to an army is in cooperating with the CIC. When the army has occupied an area, the OSS men who have been working there under cover can join forces with the CIC staff, who are new in the area and presumably ignorant of local conditions, and they can then spend some time breaking in the CIC men and introducing them to their contacts, providing the contacts can be transferred—sometimes the ties are so personal that these contacts will not be shifted.

In the Fifth Army, Lieutenant Colonel William B. Parsons was in charge of the CIC. He appreciated the work that the OSS men had done in that area, and gave all support and encouragement to Staff Reid, Gordon Browne, and myself. He let us take his men on jobs, he let me use Captain Bourgoin, whom he had taken over from the OSS, he let us use his civilian cars, he gave me the use of a Military Intelligence badge, which saved me many embarrassing explanations, and in general he was extremely kind and cooperative. In return we did all that we could for him and for his men.

Colonel Parsons had the idea that the CIC might function better if it were a part of OSS instead of G-2; there is much to be said for this theory. Ideally CIC takes over where OSS leaves off, and there must be a close relationship between the two if the CIC is to start functioning efficiently from the moment it moves into an area. In Oran the CIC staff under Captain Reed would have been lost without Leland Rounds; in Casa the same is true in the case of Stafford Reid. In any case, whatever the eventual status of CIC, it must have this OSS overlap as it had in the Fifth Army area. Furthermore, many of the CIC men would be much better off if they had had OSS type of training, instead of or in addition to the G-Man legal type of training they received.

Another reason why it might be a good idea for OSS to take CIC away from G-2 is that, in the North African theater at least, G-2 is dominated by SIS, of which more later.

It is a somewhat anomalous situation to have OSS men and CIC men working at the same problems in the same area; given less agreeable personalities than that of Colonel Parsons this duplication might lead to conflict. My suggestions are: That if OSS men want to stay in an area occupied by the army after the period needed to break in the CIC men, they should join the CIC; otherwise the general standard of the CIC should be raised to include men of OSS caliber and training. CIC does contain such men; for example, Walcott, Emmett, and Haseltine, all of the Oujda staff, as well as Porter in Fez, are extremely competent, high-caliber men; they should have the benefit of OSS training and the freedom which OSS men enjoy. In any case, *the relationship between OSS and CIC should be defined so that potential conflicting situations may be avoided.*

Navy. I have had little experience with the relations between the OSS and the navy, except that in Tangier the OSS office operated under the cover of the naval attaché's office, and Colonel Eddy used the assistant naval attachés and the two chief yeomen (later warrant officers) in our work. Also in Algiers our communications were in the hands of naval personnel. As far as I have seen the relationship between the OSS and the navy has been a peculiarly happy one, and I think credit for this belongs as much to Colonel Eddy as to the navy.

Marine Corps. Maritime Corps cover seems a particularly felicitous arrangement for OSS men. Marines are commandos by tradition and training; they have the flexibility and individual initiative and responsibility needed for OSS work. Furthermore, in a predominantly army environment, a Marine is not as subject to restrictions as an army officer of equal rank.

All of our men who were marines have done outstandingly good work, and this applies to Captain Ortiz and Lieutenant Harris as well as to Colonel Eddy himself and Captain Holcomb.

The Marine Corps is a small enough and personal enough organization to provide just that degree of elasticity which we need in our cover jobs. Personally I think that, as far as my limited experience allows me to judge, marine cover is the best obtainable. A marine uniform looks like an army uniform and in an inland country is not as conspicuous as a navy uniform; furthermore, marines go everywhere while sailors are supposed to stick reasonably close to the sea.

State Department. In the days before the landing only three kinds of cover were possible—military attaché, naval attaché, and State Department. We had no men in the military attaché's office, since that belonged to G-2 and G-2 was not in on the local preparations for the landing. Only a very few agents could use the naval attaché cover, and hence the rest had to be State Department. Any other kind of cover would have been either too easily revealed or too inflexible. Americans were not allowed in North Africa in any other role; any other cover would have involved concealing one's American nationality.

Our relations with the State Department can be divided into two categories; our relations with Bob Murphy and all others. Since Murphy was in reality one of us, and shared with Colonel Eddy the responsibility for the preparations for the landing, our relations with him were naturally always very cordial and open. He and his "food control" vice-consuls worked along with us from the beginning. One of his food-control men, Gordon Browne, was OSS from the beginning; others became OSS. Canfield after he came home, and King, Reid, Rounds, Knight, and Springs on the spot. Eddy's method of recruiting men on the spot who had the local knowledge and the requisite ability was a particularly fortunate one. Without King, Reid, Rounds, Knight, and Springs the landing could not have been engineered. I was the only fully trained OSS man sent out on that job; Browne, who preceded me by several weeks, was only partly trained, and had to learn his demolition at Gibraltar.

Our relations with the rest of the State Department were not always as felicitous as those named above. Childs, Russell, and Doolittle did not know what we were doing. They knew that we were up to some kind of tricks, but they did not know what tricks. Naturally they sometimes hindered us from important activities through their failure to understand what these were. Some of the younger men resented us; one career vice-consul in Casablanca told Auer (this is recorded in an official report to the State Department) when Auer asked him about all the vice-consuls, "Some of them don't know much about consular work." Others wanted to join us.

After the initial surprise of the landing, most of them took it like good sports; only one held it against us for not having told him about it. As far as I know he still holds it against us.

After all, the State Department is in the position of ancient heralds, who wore special costumes, carried special insignia, and could pass anywhere in hostile or friendly territory. The inviolability of the herald is found in all human societies at all times; even the Australian aborigines send heralds between tribes. In order to be inviolable the herald must follow a very circumscribed pattern of behavior; if he misbehaves he loses his status and his inviolability. It is the same with Moslem living saints; they cannot be harmed by any believer, but at the same time they cannot fight; they must observe the religious taboos more strictly than ordinary men. Hence if the members of the State Department were alarmed to see us as berserks in heralds' clothing, we had no right to be surprised; it was our job to disturb them as little as possible and be as pleasant to them as we could. The State Department conditions its men to a way of thinking that is very circumscribed, just as the religious profession does and the professional army as well. Our posing as diplomats was just as anomalous a situation as if we had posed as priests.

For these reasons I would not like to use State Department cover again if there were any other cover available which permitted equal freedom of movement. However, I am very grateful to the State Department for having allowed me to disguise myself in its vestments.

The SOE. Probably one of the happiest unions in the history of international relations was that which existed, and still exists, between OSS and our British counterpart, the SOE. In my experience we worked in complete harmony and unison. Any difficulties that arose, and they were very few, were between individuals, regardless of nationality, and not between nationalities. Colonel Eddy was (and is) head of all OSS-SOE work in the North African theater. He was thus over Colonel Brian Clark of Gibraltar and his staff, and over Lieutenant Colonel Anstruthers in Tunisia, and over the Massingham show in Algiers. He got along very well with all of them. I have been attached to all three of these groups at one time or another, and have found them extremely cooperative and hospitable. Also in Tangier our relationship with Edward Tigar, the SOE man there, and his staff was so close that we were virtually united.

Major General Gubbins, who came out from England as the leader of SOE, is a man of extraordinarily fine personality and he was very kind and considerate to all of us. All in all I may say that I have never met anywhere a finer group of men than the SOE outfit, and that I would consider it a privilege and a pleasure to go anywhere and take on any job with them.

The SIS. Unfortunately I cannot say the same for SIS. This British intelligence service holds itself aloof from the SOE as from us, and it is a question whether the worst enemy of the SOE is the Germans or the SIS. In Tangier the SIS was headed by Colonel Ellis, a man of no scruples, universally detested by British, Americans, Arabs, and everyone else. There would be no point in my listing his malefactions here; all I need say for the record is that our relations with him were formal, aloof, and mistrustful. He tried on several occasions to impede our operations, and if he had succeeded he might have completely ruined our preparations for the landing and given the show away.

Another SIS man who is our enemy is Lieutenant Colonel Hill-Dillon of G-2 in Algiers, who has charge of security for the AFHQ. He has tried on several occasions to upset our shows; he stormed into our headquarters at Jebel Halluf and accused Hamish Torrance and myself of nefarious actions, but we slapped it back at him and proved to him that he had no ground for complaint. I have it on good but unquotable authority that it was he who prevented one of our greatest strategists, Colonel Rattay, from seeing action at the front, and that it was he who kept Colonel Parsons from being head of the CIC at AFHQ, because he told Parsons that he must communicate through Captain Park, a ratlike British SIS agent in Casablanca. Despite the fact that SIS has agreed to stay out of the Fifth Army area, they keep filtering in, and Park and the rest should be removed.

All SIS men are not of the same color; Lieutenant Colonel Malcolm Henderson, who served under Ellis in Tangier while under the cover of military attaché, was a fine fellow and cooperated fully with us; in turn we gave him all information to which we thought he was entitled. Captain David Thompson, who has taken over Henderson's job, is also a fine fellow; Colonel Codrington of Gibraltar is friendly and cooperative also; Marcel, the SIS undercover man in Oran, who is supposed to be a French farmer, is in the same category. Both Henderson and Marcel have expressed the desire to quit SIS and work for OSS, which unfortunately cannot be done for reasons of nationality and because they are commissioned in the British Army.

If SIS is to control G-2, then we must give G-2 a wide berth. SIS is an imperialistic organization closely tied in with the Foreign office, and together they form the only British outfit which, in my opinion, we have any reason to mistrust.

The French. One cannot generalize about the French, except to say that no two are alike. Hence our relations with the French rest on an individualistic basis. Before the landing I had nothing to do with them; this was the work of Colonel Eddy, Bob Murphy, Dave King, and others; hence I have no remarks to make. My only experience with them other than as a soldier fell during my period of service with the Fifth Army, and I found at that time that I could deal with individuals of the rank of captain or lower easily and freely; that they could be made to cooperate, and most of them were on our side. With majors and higher I had less success. I hope, however, that I will not in the future have to deal with them too often because I find them extremely tiring; they talk incessantly and at great speed and completely without organization, and I find that after two or three hours my attention wanders and I have a tendency to get up and pace around the room.

I think, however, that the OSS men concerned with the French did their jobs extremely well; the way Murphy handled Giraud, the way Dave King handled his men at Casa, and Knight's extremely understanding way with them, to give a few examples, must constitute one of the most outstanding feats of diplomacy in recent history.

The Question of Cover. The question of cover is one that can only be settled by experience. We have had, however, enough experience to determine a few principles. There are two things good cover should avoid; tying the agent down with cover activities, and making him conspicuous. In Tangier Waller Booth uses a petroleum cover. As a result he got in close contact with the Spaniards and they do not, I believe, yet know that he is an agent. From these points of view his cover is excellent. On the other hand, this oil business keeps him so busy that he has little time for his SI work, and hence he is up most of the night and wears himself out; furthermore, he must go where the oil business takes him and not where his SI work would indicate.

State Department cover is good in that it allows the agent to go places where he could not otherwise get; it does not take up too much of his time. It is bad in that he is conspicuous and constantly under enemy surveillance. They undoubtedly know he is an agent, but don't dare harm him in neutral territory. This simply means that the agent has to be particularly careful while meeting his men. In Morocco Browne and I met dozens of people dozens of times without being caught; not even the French authorities knew whom we were seeing. But we had to work hard to do this.

In territory occupied by allied armies, State Department cover is unnecessary and one's civilian status is conspicuous. When the agent is doing very undiplomatic business, to explain that one is a State Department official gives one away immediately. Thus for me to call myself a State Department man in either Tunisia or Oujda would have been ridiculous. In Tunisia I was (when possible) a British soldier, in Oujda a member of the CIC.

Special civilian covers are useful only for special jobs of brief duration. Thus to be a war correspondent is no good in general, since a war correspondent has to follow the armies and send in his dispatches; it limits him too much spatially and takes too much of his time. But if a single job is to be done in a specific place, a special war correspondent might conceivably be sent for a single special story, do his job, and go home. Still this is not very good.

To be an archaeologist is silly, even if the agent is really a well-known professional archaeologist in peace time. All archaeologists are inevitably suspected of being agents anyhow even in peace time; and who cares about archaeology in wartime? An archaeologist may be very useful for his knowledge of the country, its people, languages, etc., but he must not pretend that he is still an archaeologist in war.

In most of the countries with which the OSS may have occasion to deal from now on, American civilians are very rare. So to be a civilian makes one immediately conspicuous and suspect. Furthermore, an American must appear important if he is to talk with important people, that is, people who are important in the local governments or in undercover organizations. He must appear important to receive the type of treatment which makes it easy for him to get around and do his work. Therefore, he needs rank and title. The best kind of rank and title which Iranians, Turks, Yugoslavs, Spaniards, and others understand is military rank. An agent who is to do a job of any consequence must be a major or better; he really should be a lieutenant colonel or colonel. That in my opinion is the best cover of all in the countries with which we may be concerned.

The only other cover I can think of in these countries would be that of a missionary, but this seems impossible because I do not believe that any mission board would let an OSS man use it as cover, nor could he get away with it without permission. Missionaries are a special breed and they could smell impostors a hundred miles away. Furthermore, Moslems do not like them.

So in general and except for very special jobs of brief duration, it is my feeling that OSS agents in Old World theaters can best use a military (army, navy, or Marine Corps) cover, on some kind of detached service or special mission, which allows the privilege of wearing civilian clothes when this is advisable. They should never go as enlisted men; the case of Sickler, narrated earlier, should be sufficient example, but the case of Byzek, Goff, Felsen, and others might be added if necessary.

There are some cases in which U.S. military or naval cover is impossible. Agents in enemy territory, or in neutral countries where the only possible cover is diplomatic, are the principal examples. But in occupied countries, in all other neutral countries, and for brief sojourns behind the lines, *all OSS agents should normally have the privilege of wearing officers' uniforms.** If the army appreciates what we have done and are doing to help them, they should make this possible, for otherwise our usefulness to them will be reduced.

* This does not of course apply to coding clerks and other office personnel, who can retain enlisted status without conflict.

C H A P T E R   S E V E N

My First and Last Commands

Biographical Setting

THROUGHOUT this book, Carleton Coon has been a civilian posing now and then as a diplomat. The Presidential Citation that follows is addressed to Major Coon of the Army. The citation spells out some things the author glosses over, but it does not explain how he got his majority. He himself does that in the short, retrospective summary at the end.

The President of the United States of America, authorized by Act of Congress July 20, 1942 has awarded the Legion of Merit to
MAJOR CARLETON S. COON, USA
for exceptionally meritorious conduct in the performance of outstanding services:

Major Carleton S. Coon, as an agent of the Office of Strategic Services, performed meritorious services in North Africa and Corsica from May 1942 to October 1943. Acting as courier between Gibraltar, Tangier and French Morocco, he smuggled firearms and explosives to French resistance groups in the areas planned for the Allied landings in November 1942, and collected vital in-

telligence material for use in the landings. Later, in Tunisia, while a member of a small group of fifty men who held twenty-eight miles of territory between Sedjanane and the sea against approximately six hundred enemy troops, Major Coon, through his superior tact and resourcefulness, won the native population to the Allied cause. On many occasions he conducted patrols into no-man's land to set booby traps and signal devices, and in addition he trained, equipped and dispatched Arab agents to a vital railway bridge which was successfully destroyed while a trainload of German troops was crossing it. Later, landing with the assault waves on Corsica, he directed the infiltration of agents who procured vital information which contributed directly to the destruction of several thousand enemy, hundreds of vehicles and several large ships during the Allied conquest of the Island. Major Coon's exceptional performance in accomplishing these missions of great importance materially advanced the Allied war effort.

Corsica and Italy 1943–1944

THE preceding chapter ends my contemporaneous record. It was not the end of my service with the OSS, which lasted until late February of 1945, a few months before the agency was dissolved. What I write now is drawn mainly from memory.

After the threat of a German invasion of North Africa had fallen to the status of a deliberately spread rumor, the allied war planners' attention turned toward an invasion across Albania from the Straits of Otranto to Lake Okhrid and thence eastward to the Aegean and the Black Sea. If successful, such an operation could pen Rommel's army in Greece and the Levant, like sheep in a fold.

Because I had explored the mountains of Northern Albania in 1929 and 1930, and made there some promising contacts, in May of 1943 I was sent home to get an army commission and to recruit Albanian agents in Boston and Brockton, Massachusetts. Getting my commission, as an infantry major, was not easy. The doctors said that I would look awkward in parades because my left leg is congenitally one inch shorter than my right one. I passed, probably because someone tipped them off that marching was not an important part of my job.

Also, the only Albanians available in Massachusetts were Toscs (South Albanians), not Ghegs(North Albanians). The former are villagers, the latter feuding tribesmen, like Riffians and traditional Scots. The men I recruited were patriotic, brave, Orthodox Christians, a minority reared among wealthier Turkophile Moslems. I was flown to Cairo, laid on our plans with the help of a British lady-explorer, Margaret Hasluck, who had also studied the Ghegs at home, and I was ready to be sent to parachute school in Haifa when a message came through from Algiers, to report to General Donovan there at once.

Bill Donovan looked at me with his pale, blue, unblinking eyes and asked me: "Carl, how would you like to go to Corsica?"

Surprised by this unexpected question, I hesitated a moment. Bill's eyes snapped.

"Yes, Bill, fine," I replied.

He gave me twenty-four hours to collect my crew and gear. Captain Elmer (Pinkie) Harris, a Norwegian-American from Washington State, was my fiendish demolition chief. John Ffoulke (born Levie), a native of Corsica, reared in the United States, knew everyone on the island. An Italian-speaking captain from Watertown, Massachusetts, commanded a whole SO (Special Operations) group of one lieutenant and about forty Abruzzi mountaineers from the Main Line between Wayne and Paoli, Pennsylvania. With all our small arms, bazookas, ammunition, and other supplies piled up on the deck of a sleek French cruiser, we boarded it in Algiers Harbor, and it ran by moonlight across the Mediterranean to Ajaccio, with Pinky and me up in the anti-aircraft turrets in the bow, where Breton sharpshooters crouched waiting for the German planes, fingering tiny bagpipes and chatting together in their own Celtic language, the language of King Arthur of the Round Table, and of my own great-great-grandparents in Cornwall. It was like Merlin casting his druid spell to keep Odin's battle-hawks at bay. What we did in Corsica is a matter of public record because newsmen soon joined us. My mother even read about it in the Wakefield, Massachusetts, *Daily Item*.

Retrospective Summary

MY next assignment was in Bari, Italy, in charge of the OSS's part in the mixup between Tito and Mihailovich, in which both the OSS and SOE were hamstrung by conflicting orders because of a change of plans at the Yalta Conference. General Colin Gubbins came into my requisitioned apartment and wept privately, not because his son Captain Michael Gubbins had been killed in northern Italy, which he took without flinching, but because another Scot had been raised from a captaincy to act over his head. My Massachusetts Albanians joined me and were sent off in small boats by night to whatever fate awaited them.

I could not keep track of them because I, too, was over the fire, and my nervous system finally collapsed, supposedly from the crack over my head at Jebel Abiodh in Tunisia. Gordon Browne, sent down from London to join the Adriatic tangle, found me in a field hospital in a ward with its floor slippery with blood. I was sent home on a Naval hospital ship from Oran. Bill Donovan sent me on secretly to Boston to have a suspected brain tumor removed. While Seagraves, the Burma surgeon, home on leave, distracted my attention with tales of the naked Nagas of his hills, Dr. Gilbert Horrox, one of America's top brain surgeons, drained my cerebrospinal fluid out through two holes in my skull, took a picture, and found no tumor. When my condition did not change, Dr. Horrox cut the nerves on the right-rear of my skull, paralyzing my right ear for many years. My health improved, but Bill Donovon did not think it good enough for further fighting.

His decision came to a head when Field Marshal Douglas MacArthur, Donovan's old rival, who outranked him by three stars, demanded that I be transferred to his command to raise a rebellion among the Moslem Moros in Mindanao in the Philippines. Bill Donovan managed to find a way to refuse this order without telling the immortal Old Soldier why.

The last time I saw General Donovan alive was in 1954 in Bangkok, Thailand, where he was serving as American ambassador. He and Ruth Donovan and Gordon and Eleanor Browne (also living there) and Lisa Coon and I were about to go riding elephants into a jungle to visit a large cave that might have an archaeological deposit in its floor. Bill sent his aide Mr. Rafferty along in his place, because a Donovan grandchild had cut his grandfather's eyeball with a glazed page of the *Saturday Evening Post.*

I went to his memorial Mass in 1959 at St. Patrick's Cathedral in New York, where his men of all faiths had gathered to pay our last homage. Some of us were a bit confused about when to kneel down and when to jump up, and wondered what all those telephone bells were incessantly ringing for.

No one answered them.

No one who could was alive.

INDEX

of Names

Index

Index

Hitler, Adolf, 10, 22, 125
Holcomb, Capt. Franklin P., 35, 129
Holcomb, Lieut. Col. Carl, 42
Hooton, Prof. Earnest A., viii
Horrox, Dr. Gilbert, 140, 141
Howard, Col. Edwin B., 72, 106, 114, 121, 122, 125
Howe, General (*Code name, see Eisenhower*), 40
Howze, Colonel, 96, 97
Huntington, Col. Ellery, 99, 101
Idris, 34
Imossi, Pepe, 49, 50
Intrepid (*Code name, see Stephenson, William*), 89
Ishaq, Cohen, 36, 37, 38, 54
Johnson, Colonel, 20, 24, 26
Kenmore, Colonel, 106
Keswick, Colonel, 56
Keyes, General, 54, 105
King, Dave, 34, 54, 56, 130, 133
King, Control Vice Consul, 5
King Ibn Sa'ud, 46
Kitts, Ensign, 41, 42
Kline, Lieutenant, 108
Knight, Vice Consul Ridgway, 56, 130, 133
Kraemer, 109, 116
Lambert, Colonel, 105
Lassowsky, Sergeant, 91, 92
Legrand, Captain (*See also Lefort*), 108, 110, 115
Lemaitre, Charlot, 68–69
Lemaitre, Edmond, 68–69
Levy, 64, 64n, 77
Litsey, Lieutenant, 48
Lovelock, Captain, 85
Lovatt, Captain, 67, 88
Lucina, 102
Luiz, 112
McAndrews, Lieutenant, 67, 68, 85, 88
MacArthur, Field Marshall Douglas, 141
McCloy, John, 101
MacCool, 94
MacFarlane, Second Lieutenant, 81

MacIntosh, Capt. Charles, 31, 33, 101
McNab, Brigadier, 99
McQuillan, General, 95, 96, 98
Mahouzies, Lieutenant, 75, 78, 81
Mallory, Squadron Leader (*See also Bombshell*), 39, 40, 65, 66
Mansouri, Kaid, 115
Mara Mara, 59
Marachi, Lieutenant, 39
Marcel, 132
Mark, General (*See Gen. Mark Clark*), 40
Marshal, 74
Massali, Hajj, 105
Massingham, 131
Matenet, 74
Mayer, Lieut. Lee, 117
Mekkwar, Si Hamid, 21, 23
Mihailovich, Gen. Draza, 89, 140
Millard, Mr., 7
Moktav, 110
Montandon, 22
Montgomery, General, 89
Morris, Haley, 40
Movius, Capt. Hallam L., 102
Mulay, Ali, 25, 27
Murphy, Robert, 12, 36, 41, 44, 47, 129, 133
Mussolini, Benito, 10, 125
Nahon, Dr. Ralph, 25
Nasiri, Mekki, 21
The Neanderthal (Big Absalem), 25
Nogues, Gen. Auguste, 15, 43, 115
O'Brien, Commander, 42
Orgaz, General, 13, 21
Ortiz, Captain, 129
Park, Captain, 132
Parsons, Lieut. Col. William B., 107, 108, 114, 115, 119, 121, 127, 128, 132
Parsons, Private, 82
Pascual, Jose, 111, 116
Patton, Gen. George, 55, 89, 103
Pendar, Control Vice Consul Kenneth, 5
Perez, Lieut. Col. Sanchez, 27
Perrin, Commandant, 73, 75, 83, 84, 85

Index